DEMANDING DEMOCRACY

Demanding Democracy

Robert Schmuhl

University of Notre Dame Press
Notre Dame   London

Library of Congress Cataloging-in-Publication Data

Schmuhl, Robert.
    Demanding democracy / Robert Schmuhl.
       p.   cm.
    Includes bibliographical references
    ISBN 0-268-00872-8 (alk. paper)
    1. Mass media—Political aspects—United States.   2. United
States—Politics and government—1989–1993.   I. Title.
P95.82.U6S347   1994
302.23'0973—dc20   93-45868
                                                                CIP

For Michael
And his generation
Of democrats

Contents

Introduction

Looking Outward

This book continues where an earlier one, *Statecraft and Stagecraft: American Political Life in the Age of Personality*, left off. Published in 1990, with a second edition in 1992, *Statecraft and Stagecraft* surveyed the political and media territory after 1968. Until the closing months of the 1992 presidential campaign, I intended to write a chapter about political media activities of that year and include it as a postscript to a third edition. However, what happened throughout 1992 proved to be not only unprecedented but revolutionary. Many of my earlier points now seemed anachronistic, pertinent to another time, overtaken by a convergence of contemporary forces that radically changed American political life. This new book attempts to chronicle many of those changes and to look ahead to a future that will be vastly different from today.

In *Statecraft and Stagecraft*, I tried to explain how "statecraft" (conducting or seeking public office) and "stagecraft" (communicating through the media messages about governing or campaigning) have become intertwined since the 1960s. Now more than ever before, our political culture and our media culture share common characteristics, traits, and values. In the worlds

1

of politics and communications, there is a democratic impulse to figure out and respond to the public—our needs and wants, our attitudes and beliefs, our dreams and nightmares. The media of stagecraft have grown in significance and prominence as has an emphasis on the political personality engaged in some aspect of statecraft. Indeed, the decline of the political parties and the rise of the individual figure occurred simultaneously. With the formal institution for candidate selection, member discipline, and public information no longer possessing that much clout, the informal institutions of popular communications, especially television, became more important intermediaries between our political life and the citizenry. We've reached the point where—in the estimation of Tim Russert, a former political insider who is now NBC's Washington bureau chief—"At least half of what a politician does every day is talk to the media, prepare to talk to the media, or read or watch the media."

In recent years, individual personalities assumed new and different stature. These self-made figures (frequently enamored of their creators) presented themselves to the public by "making news" or "buying time." What they did that was transmitted by the media frequently meant the difference between winning and losing, governing or not. This phenomenon of the media-oriented political personality is evident at local, state, and national levels of government. In both 1976 and 1992, two relatively unknown Southern governors won the White House by conducting effective campaigns with heavy reliance on the various forms of popular communication. Jimmy Carter and Bill Clinton became president despite the reservations of so-called party leaders and their virtual anonymity a year before the election.

But the intertwining of statecraft and stagecraft goes well beyond the conduct of individual personalities involved in American political life. The media send messages that promote or shape policy measures. Coverage of the inhuman treatment of the Kurds in northern Iraq in 1991 and of the mass starvation in Somalia in 1992 helped pushed the administration of George Bush to take action. When Bill Clinton approved the firing of missiles against Iraq for allegedly plotting to assassinate former president Bush during a visit to Kuwait in the spring of 1993, one factor might have made the military operation more successful. The first paragraph of a piece of news analysis in *The New York Times* reported, "White House officials said today that their only regret about the missile attack on the Iraqi intelligence headquarters was that there was no CNN [Cable News Network] crew there to broadcast the event live so it could be watched in the Sudan, Iran and other countries suspected of involvement in terrorism." In an age of instantaneous, worldwide communication, the media affect policy formulation and implementation. Today diplomatic messages frequently arrive via the television screen instead of from an ambassador or courier. Reports have different audiences and can produce varying effects both at home and abroad. The media might try to simplify knotty reality to make it understandable for the average citizen, but the consequences of that simplification are complex and never easy to gauge.

The interplay between political life and popular communications was so frenetic during 1992 that it was difficult for the public to keep up. Despite being breathless and often bewildered, the people showed what could happen if they demonstrated civic interest and involvement. As if overnight, the political dialogue changed. The ten-second sound bite and thirty-second spot, which had been the principal currency of political communication in recent years, were not only overshadowed but replaced in significance by longer, more probing formats, such as talk shows, discussion programs, and debates.

A month before the election, Jonathan Alter, a perceptive commentator on politics and the media for *Newsweek*, noted, "It is my sense this year that there were essentially two rebellions in American politics. One was a rebellion against politics as usual, and then there was a second rebellion against media as usual. And they were part of the same phenomenon."[1] The people, of course, were behind both rebellions, pushing the political and communication establishments into new, previously uncharted territory. The infatuation with independent presidential candidate Ross Perot in the spring and his winning nearly twenty million votes (19 percent) on election day symbolized one aspect of the rebellion. The sizable television audiences for extended candidate discussions typified the other.

The title of this book, *Demanding Democracy*, describes not only what we saw happening in 1992, but what I foresee occurring in the years to come. There's a growing sense in America that our political life of campaigning and governing has become remote from the people. Insiders, whether in politics, political action committees, or the press, do their work at a distance that irritates some citizens and infuriates others. According to this perspective, public business excludes public involvement. Where is the necessary accountability? What type of say does the average person have? Who is responsible for all of the festering sores on the body politic?

To reduce the troubling distance, the people seem willing to consider or to try any number of alternatives. Setting term limits for elected officials is one remedy that's gaining greater popularity. Opening the political process to accommodate more easily people outside the two traditional parties is another activity. Creating a more direct, democratic system by using interactive, two-way communication technology is the answer in the opinion of more and more citizens. Common to these and other approaches is a sincerity to do something definite and dramatically different that restores the body politic, indeed the country, to healthful vigor.

One of the most popular books during the 1992 political season was *America: What Went Wrong?* The question of the title implies both departure from the past and a sense of national loss. People today are groping to find ways to put America back on track, and that means greater public pressure on any and all institutions deemed at fault or thought to be potentially helpful in correcting the problems. Those in public service feel the pressure the most; however, given the centrality of the media in the political realm, people in communications regularly experience the ire of the electorate, too. If the recent past is any guide, citizens will maneuver around established institutions and figures in both politics and communications as they demand democracy that's more proximate and participatory.

Scandalously heterodox or unduly unpatriotic as it might sound, democracy is similar to pornography—easier to identify than to define. The Greek roots—*demos* (people) and *kratos* (rule)—offer the foundation for any definition, but American democracy has been a continuing experiment over more than two hundred years in figuring out which people will rule and what precise role they will play in this system. Seven of the sixteen amendments to the Constitution since the passage of the Bill of Rights broaden voting rights or give more direct electoral involvement, reflecting formal, sustained efforts to include more people in our so-called "democratic experience." That, for instance, woman's suffrage was advocated for decades but didn't become law until 1920 is a telling example of another aspect of democracy. Open debate and demonstration (in the words of the First Amendment

"freedom of speech, or of the press; or the right of the
people peaceably to assemble, and to petition the
Government for a redress of grievances") are also possible in America without having the voting franchise,
making democracy much more than the casting of ballots.
Freedom, the cornerstone of American political culture,
animates the democratic spirit, becoming part of the air
we breathe.

Although democracy is considerably more than the
presumably informed citizenry going to vote every so
often, it is also much less than the people actually ruling.
Political thinkers scrupulously make the distinction
between a democracy and a republic. According to *The
Federalist Papers* (Number 10), "a pure democracy"
means "a society consisting of a small number of citizens, who assemble and administer the government in
person. . . ." With "a republic" you have "the delegation
of the government . . . to a small number of citizens
elected by the rest. . . ." In America, however, the Founders' distinction has lost much of its relevance over time.

George F. Kennan might not be alone when he says,
"The words 'democracy' and 'democratic' have, in short,
been so extensively abused as to be deprived of any very
clear meaning; and the employment of them in public
discussion merely encourages the sloppy imprecision of
language that runs through so much of American political discourse and literature."[2] But the phrases "American
democracy" and, thanks to Tocqueville, "Democracy in
America" have over time gained such power that defi-
nitional details and quibbles now seem a pillow fight
among pedants. In an unofficial yet democratically determining way, the people have decided that the word
democracy is their descriptive choice. The people's decision is reflected in what those in political life and in the
media say. Running for president, Bill Clinton spoke seriously about "the great mystery of American democracy,"

appropriating an ironic phrase from Henry Adams (in his 1880 novel *Democracy* Adams's character Mrs. Lightfoot Lee is "bent upon getting to the heart of the great American mystery of democracy and government"). Rush Limbaugh, with characteristic modesty, refers to himself as "the doctor of democracy." Headlines use such phrases as "sound-bite democracy," "talk-show democracy," "townhall democracy," and "video democracy."

American history is testament to the core beliefs embedded in this much-used word. The universe of potential voters has expanded tremendously, and the proliferation of primaries and caucuses since the 1960s has created what might be considered direct democracy (in the selection of political candidates) leading to representative democracy (the conduct of government by candidates winning a majority of the votes).[3] A critical concern in the future will be whether to extend democracy even further by using the sophisticated communications technology that will be widely available.

One reason we've seen an expanding democracy and allegiance to the word is the shared faith in the wisdom of citizens to do what is right for themselves and others. In words and pictures, Americans affirm what they perceive as their role, rights, and responsibilities. The opening phrase of the preamble to the Constitution is "We the People," with a capital P. In *Democratic Vistas* Walt Whitman begins a paragraph, "The People!" and refers to "the pride and dignity of the common people, the lifeblood of democracy." Carl Sandburg's most enduring work of poetry carries the title *The People, Yes.* Popular films—everything from "Mr. Smith Goes to Washington" to "Dave"—strike similar chords and feature ordinary, average, typical or common citizens becoming involved in democratic action that's both personally ennobling and publicly beneficial. Many of the most famous paintings of that All-American artist Norman Rockwell visually offer an identical message. To be sure, we're dealing here with a world of romance and myth, but there's a strong enough connection to reality that we accept the basic premises as how we are—or at least how we would like to be.

The "we," by and large, means citizens of middlebrow tastes and middle-class lifestyles. They anchor America, and give the country a constancy that people elsewhere admire. Concern for politics and government is not so much a preoccupation as a way of everyday life. Kevin Phillips remarks in *Boiling Point*, "From the frontier vitality of Jacksonian Democracy in 1828 to the electoral revolution of 1992, ordinary Americans—whether they be called yeomanry, the 'middling sort' or twentieth-century middle class—have made the U.S. system of politics and government one of the world's most effective. It is they who have made democracy work."[4] But throughout 1992, there was an unsettling feeling that democracy was in jeopardy and that the people had to do something to take things in their own hands. The subtitle of William Greider's best-selling book *Who Will Tell the People* captured the mood of the campaign year: *The Betrayal of American Democracy*.

For anyone following American political life in 1992, the most common (and continuing) reaction was head-shaking disbelief. That tabloid report says what? A punch-in-the-nose pundit can't be a serious presidential candidate, can he? The vice president is worried about which television show? How many tuned in to see the thirty-minute political infomercial? The questions and answers, rumors and revelations, twists and turns aroused citizen interest but also signified a nervous and anxious nation. People weren't sure about tomorrow because today seemed so different from yesterday. Politics is humanly unpredictable, yet what was happening had no precedents to help someone better understand such a turbulent year.

Since so little that occurred followed conventional patterns and practices, the very idea of "conventional wisdom" quickly became suspect. With so much taking place that is unconventional and history not much of a guide, conventional wisdom is not that different from idle speculation. An irony of our information age is that multiple sources require ever more material to fill their time and space. Frequently, however, instead of illuminating a subject, commentators offer guesses or personal impressions that don't hold up and actually obscure the meaning of the situation. A simple "I don't know" is out of the question because that response weakens the status of the so-called expert, and it also doesn't do much to fill either the time or space.

With conventional wisdom proving so unenlightening in 1992, citizens found other ways of measuring the candidates and making decisions about the issues. As will be explained later, the people drove much of what happened throughout the year. Talk shows and the debates allowed the electorate to assess the candidates for sustained periods. The communication was more direct and less filtered. Commentators were free to guess and to spin their analytical webs, but in the public mind what they were saying was so much chatter without much import. They were sideshow performers (in some cases almost clown-like), while the people focused their attention on the main event.

The stones being cast at "experts" might just as well be boomerangs. With the publication of *Statecraft and Stagecraft* and a number of fugitive essays, my name found its way to the "dial-a-quote" directory of some reporters and producers. In print and over the air, I've been referred to as "a political scientist," "a debate expert," and (in *Harper's* no less) an academic "who specializes in the country's peculiar fascination with personality politics." One newspaper even used the intriguing label "political professor." To be perfectly clear and in a spirit of full disclosure, I am not (and have never been) a political scientist, debate expert, or a specialist in personality politics. I teach in an interdisciplinary department of American studies after graduate training in literature and American studies. Employment in journalism, politics, and government along the way offered real-world experience to balance, and actually augment, the book-learning. Schooling didn't get in the way of my education, as Mark Twain thought it did for him, yet I remain as attracted to a newsroom or campaign headquarters as a library. Although any active partisan involvement came to an end when I started to do political commentary, I see journalistic work and analysis with footnotes as worthwhile activities of political life.

Ronald Reagan saw himself as a "citizen-politician," with presumably an emphasis on the one-among-many, democratic designation of citizen before a specific role or type of work. When pressed, I describe myself as a "citizen-critic," with a similar emphasis on the first word and the second suggesting a particular perspective of interpretation and evaluation. More generalist than specialist (a heinous admission for an academic today), I watch American political life from a vantage point in the center of the country and try to look at public affairs and figures in much the same way as a representative voter or taxpayer might.

This stance, I confess, did not keep me from saying things in 1992 as laughably misguided as someone working within the Washington Beltway. In a mid-February interview, I had enough sense to say 1992 was a "year that cries out for substance," but went on to remark that the Democrats have "gone from having someone who quickly emerged as the likely front-runner [Bill Clinton] to someone around whom many serious questions swirl, so many, in fact, that Clinton's candidacy is very much in doubt." Eight months later, after Ross Perot had gotten into the presidential race, withdrawn, and returned, a wire service report carried a quotation that missed Perot's genuine following—on Election Day and subsequently: "In many respects he [Perot] remains a political sideshow. Perot lights up our televisions, but upon sober reflection people will look beyond the one liners and realize that it takes much more than effective platform talents to run the federal government." I also hopelessly misgauged the appeal of the three presidential debates, which showed sustained audience fascination instead of declining viewership. Two days before the first debate, I told a newspaper reporter: "I think there's a chance of overloading the citizenry's circuits. There'll be such wall-to-wall coverage, some people after a while will turn away out of subject fatigue. That's why God created VCRs."

Fortunately other efforts of analysis proved more accurate, but I still laugh at myself for doing a long interview with a reporter for a newsmagazine who wanted to know why I thought George Bush had come from behind to win his second term. A week before the election, with polls showing a tightening race, journalists scrambled to be ready with how-it-happened commentary. I confess: Vanity made me do it.

During the spring, summer, and fall of 1992, I offered classes that focused on the campaign and the political mood in the country. To the dismay of students, the teacher always seemed to have more questions than answers. At almost every turn something would happen to cast doubt on an assumption or a line of inquiry. It was like being trapped in a gargantuan maze, where dead ends exceeded access points by what seemed a margin of a hundred to one. Moreover, students weren't that much help in figuring out what might happen and its meaning. In fact, one experience with a student contributed to my already much-confused state.

A young woman, faithful in attending class meetings but hesitant to speak, called one day and said, "Pat Buchanan is coming to campus Tuesday. Could I cut class to go hear him speak?"

The sincerity of the request bespoke a determination that a professorial denial couldn't influence. However, I responded that my plan was to conclude Tuesday's session early, allowing all the students in the upper-level seminar about "Politics, Policy, and the Media" to attend the speech.

"I want to get there early to get a good seat," she countered. Having no prior inkling of her political allegiance, I reasoned that she must have been a member of Buchanan's dwindling faithful. He was visiting Notre Dame during the third week of April to campaign for the Indiana primary on May 5. By this time George Bush was well on his way to the Republican nomination, but Buchanan was continuing to pinball around the country rallying conservatives and staking out some territory for the future.

In the student's scheme of things, a personal visit from *her* candidate was potentially more memorable than whatever might happen in the seminar, so I ended the conversation, "Well, I guess we'll just see you there." Hanging up, I thought to myself that at least one student seemed genuinely excited about a presidential candidate in 1992, albeit one without a chance.

At the speech the next day, I saw the student sitting in the front row, applauding vigorously throughout. When it came time for questions, her hand shot up and she stood up. She inquired about the status of Buchanan's campaign with concern and poise.

Except for musing that I now knew she wasn't quite as timid as I suspected, I didn't give her action a second thought—that is, until a week later when she called again. "Jerry Brown is going to have a rally at noon tomorrow here. Could I miss class to go see him?"

Now I was profoundly perplexed. Clearly, my analysis of her true-believer allegiance to Buchanan had been faulty. But what prompted this political ambidexterity, rightward leaning one week, leftward the next?

For a second time I told her the entire class would have a chance to hear what the former California governor had to say, adding that he was notorious for arriving late at campaign events. It didn't make much sense to miss another class just to wait around, I offered somewhat sternly, hoping that the tone, if not the fact, would sway her.

"But I want to be right in front," she responded, adding "Did you see me on TV at the Buchanan rally? I was on all the local stations and CNN. They had shots of the audience. I was in all of them."

Now wait a minute, I thought to myself. Did she say TV? A light went on. It was a small red one.

At Brown's speech, which began a half-hour after its advertised time, I watched the student (strategically positioned in the front) as much as the candidate. Any time a TV mini-cam panned the crowd she held a "Brown in '92" placard above her head, moving it from side to side to give the scene some action.

During the question period, she kept her arm elevated and waving until Brown seemed obliged to recognize her. She asked about his plan for helping college students pay for their education with utmost sincerity. To be sure, in the jargon of the tube, she "made" the coverage of the event that evening—and told me about it in detail after the next seminar session.

For over a decade, I've preached to classes that television changes whatever it touches, including politics, government, and other aspects of American life. For good or ill, the presence of the most dominant medium of our time alters how people act and even how they see what's being broadcast. The reality of experience itself can change if the camera's point of view becomes our own. When perception and reality dance together, it's hard to tell which one is leading. The effects of television on what's being covered and on the viewing audience are highly variable, but all my reading of analytical treatises hadn't prepared me for this up-close and personal case study of 1992.

Why does a shy, reserved student, blessed with a fine mind, turn into an any-candidate-will-do cheerleader when cameras are around? Have we reached the point where a person thinks: I'm on TV, therefore I am? Are politicians in the television age a species of celebrity not that different from a prime-time personality or MTV marvel? And, if so, what does that perception mean over the long term? Will the people who form the public easily lose interest and become bored—and look for another engaging personality—in the random way they select television fare?

Such larger questions flow from this small anecdote. They and it were typical of the difficulty facing any watcher of political life in 1992. Uncertainty was the only certainty. It was a year for noisily breaking conventions that will have reverberations for the rest of the century and beyond.

Part One

Looking Backward

Understanding the political year of 1992 in all of its discombobulating unpredictability requires a retreat to the past, specifically to 1988 and that year's presidential campaign between George Bush and Michael Dukakis. Bush convincingly won the election, but how he reached the White House left the public—and the news media—with a bitter aftertaste that never really went away. The negative nature of the campaign had been so unpleasant it was as though the people and the press had made a pact: 1992 will be different. It certainly was. Attack ads and slashing sound bites might have been influential in 1988, but they had little impact four years later. There was a yearning for detailed statements about solving problems bedeviling America. The question "What will *you* do?" took precedence in the public mind. What was said about an opponent was a secondary or even tertiary concern.

Throughout 1992, journalism reflected a citizenry in high dudgeon. The temper of the time was distemper, and certain words recurred in the reporting: alienation, anger, anxiety, cynicism, disaffection, discontent, disenchantment, disillusionment, dissatisfaction, distrust, fear, frustration, fury, hostility, revulsion. In just four years, the country had moved from what Garry Wills termed the "Feelgood Era" of Ronald Reagan to a national funk. A French newspaper said Americans weren't conducting a campaign so much as throwing a tantrum. How had the political climate changed so dramatically?

A number of different factors, one after the other, contributed to the sour state of the public. The sterile-yet-muddy '88 campaign was one reason. The controversial pay-raise maneuvering by Congress in 1989 elevated the electorate's blood pressure, with one survey measuring 85 percent in opposition. That same year, Speaker of the House Jim Wright and House Democratic Whip Tony Coelho resigned in the wake of serious questions about their conduct of financial affairs. The 1990 mid-term elections took their cues from the 1988 presidential race and featured an endless round of negative commercials, further disgusting the public. In 1991, the Senate's confirmation hearings of Clarence Thomas for the Supreme Court raised the issue of sexual harassment, but also turned many stomachs and made certain senators look like buffoons. A few months later, the bank scandal in the House of Representatives became known, making heads shake once again over the conduct of holders of high office.

With political life reeling from such blows—all dutifully covered by the news media and ripe subjects for the growing format of talk radio—the economy was suffering from problems that threatened the country's backbone, the vital, animating middle class. Increasing numbers of people felt the so-called "downturn" in economic life. In its special election issue after the 1992 campaign, *Newsweek* summarized the realities facing millions of Americans as they voted that November:

> For the disaffected, each day's news seemed to bring fresh grounds for unbelief. The sputtering economy was itself a daily indictment, of Congress as

well as the president. The national debt had quad-
rupled in the Reagan-Bush years, to $4 trillion and
counting. Savings and loans lay in ruin. Banks were
wobbling under backlogs of bad debt. Real-estate
values crumbled. Corporations shored up profits
by "downsizing," which sounded nicer than letting
people go; blue- and white-collar jobs were disap-
pearing not just for the duration but for good. One
American in 10 was on food stamps, one in eight
living in poverty; unemployment had touched one
family in four. For those who were working, household incomes were stuck where they were in the early
'70s—and then only because the working wife had
become an American norm.

Adding to the woes of the public were social and
cultural problems or conditions that were not only troubling but frightening, especially in their implications for
the future. Alarming statistics revealed the tremendous
increase in violent crime, persistent drug and alcohol
abuse, growing numbers of out-of-wedlock births and
children with single mothers, and the rise in teen suicide.
No numerical studies were required to see the urban
decay, infrastructure disrepair, conspicuous homelessness, chaotic schools, health care problems, and the
emphasis on messages reveling in portrayals of gruesome
violence and sex-for-sex's-sake throughout the media.
Taken together, the political, economic, social, and
cultural ills created a grumpy and restless electorate in
1992. People wondered what had happened—in many
instances to them individually and more generally to
the country as a whole. Public opinion polls abounded
throughout the year and reflected unsettled minds about
candidates and their programs. However, surveys measuring whether America was going in the right or wrong
direction remained consistent. Upwards of 70 percent

said the country was on the wrong track. Yet looking more deeply at some of the data frequently left a person somewhat puzzled. Five months before the election, Yankelovich Clancy Shulman conducted a poll for *Time/CNN* that included these questions and results:

Is the country better off than it was four years ago?

Yes	*No*	*The same*
15%	72%	10%

Are you personally better off?

Yes	*No*	*The same*
39%	33%	27%

(*Time*, July 27, 1992)

The level of "consumer confidence" was faithfully reported each month, and it plummeted from a reading of 82 in March 1991 (right after the Persian Gulf War) to a reading of 56 a year later. Increasingly it became clear that embedded in "consumer confidence" is what might be called "citizen confidence"—how people think and feel about their country as a whole, its current condition, and future prospects. The mythological but powerful "American Dream" seemed more remote than before, and in the rarefied air of academia a stormy debate about "American decline" pitted "declinists" against "revivalists." Some commentators made a distinction between the "crisis of confidence" of the 1970s, which was focused more directly on governmental institutions and their working or lack thereof, and that of the early 1990s, which seemed driven by a fear of the future and the life chances or prospects awaiting aging Baby Boomers and their children. The seventy-fifth anniversary issue of the business magazine *Forbes* (September 14, 1992) was anything but celebratory. The cover package of essays by such writers as Saul Bellow, John Updike, Alfred Kazin, Henry Louis Gates, Jr., and Peggy Noonan examined "Why We Feel So Bad."

Timing is everything in politics, we're often reminded; but the times themselves are terribly important in creating a political climate. Well before the presidential campaign of 1992 began in earnest, there were numerous signs that the people and the media wanted it to be a serious examination of what ailed the country and detailed discussion about how to get back on the right track.

- In conference after conference, journalists, academics, and public-spirited citizens (some previously in politics) gathered to consider specific ways of making campaigns more substantive.
- At the beginning of 1990, the premier political writer in the country, David S. Broder of *The Washington Post*, launched his own campaign "to get some sanity back into our elections." In March of that year, *The New York Times* published a four-part series, "The Trouble With Politics," followed a few months later by the *Chicago Tribune* offering five lengthy articles about "the strains on the political process in America."
- National magazines got involved in the effort to reinvigorate political life. The lead article of *Harper's* in November 1990 was Lewis H. Lapham's sobering essay, "Democracy in America?" and the cover story of *Newsweek* for its October 14, 1991 issue was devoted to "No Bull: The Campaign America Needs—But Won't Get."
- Books, too, played a significant role. *Why Americans Hate Politics* by E. J. Dionne, Jr., and *Feeding Frenzy:*

How Attack Journalism Has Transformed American Politics by Larry J. Sabato appeared in 1991 and gained large audiences, indicating people were interested enough about the state of politics and political journalism to devote hours of reading to these subjects. During 1992, more books probing these concerns (William Greider's *Who Will Tell the People: The Betrayal of American Democracy*, Richard N. Goodwin's *Promises to Keep*, and even Tom Wicker's racy novel *Donovan's Wife*) came out and reflected a market for political works many observers found surprising.

The efforts occurring on a number of fronts—what's been mentioned just scratches the surface—indicated a broad willingness to wrestle with political problems. The public seemed receptive to detailed assessments and analyses. How people reacted to the publication in *The Philadelphia Inquirer* of the nine-part series *America: What Went Wrong?* by Donald L. Barlett and James B. Steele is a case study in the seriousness of the citizenry going into the election. Originally appearing between October 20–28, 1991, the articles struck a chord in Philadelphia and Pennsylvania as well as other parts of the country when the syndicated version ran in fifty more newspapers. After *The Inquirer* announced the availability of the series in a special section, requests poured in and ultimately reached 400,000. In addition, there were some 20,000 letters and calls reacting to the issues raised. An expanded version of *America: What Went Wrong?* appeared in book form in March 1992 and quickly made best-seller lists, where it remained for eight months (from April through November). The publisher, Andrews and McMeel, printed 500,000 copies of the book.

Remarkable reportage and analysis, *America: What Went Wrong?* provides a portrait of our political and economic system going at breakneck speed while being off the tracks. Barlett and Steele examine "the relentless shrinking of the middle class" and also explain why the 1980s and early 1990s rewarded some people with stretch-limo wealth at the same time others struggled to achieve a modest standard of living. Jobs are lost, health insurance plans cut, and pensions abandoned as companies are bought and sold in what seems a real-life Monopoly game. Blame for the country's economic plight and its dislocating consequences points, according to the authors, in two directions—toward "the lawmakers in Washington and the dealmakers on Wall Street."

The clever manipulation of the Washington "rule book" is largely at fault for the situation, with money flowing from vested interests to the politicians for their campaign expenses helping to make sure the same cozy system continues to operate. As Barlett and Steele make painfully clear, the state of the economy is entwined with political and governmental decision making: "That rule book is responsible for the decline of America's middle class, for the triumph of special interests. It determines whether you have a job that pays $15 an hour or one that pays $6; whether you have a pension and health-care insurance; whether you can afford a home. It governs everything from the tax system to imports of foreign goods, from the bankruptcy system to regulatory oversight."[1] The original series and the subsequent book proposed definite changes, but just as importantly they contributed to the more purposeful political discourse that helped shape the conduct of the campaign. Candidates, including Bill Clinton and Ross Perot, mentioned *America: What Went Wrong?* in speeches, while television and radio programs devoted hours of discussion to the work. People were coming to a better understanding of the relationship between the economic problems affecting or surrounding them and the political system that seemed unduly remote from average citizens while menacingly close to specific interests with their deep pockets of money.

The focused attention of the public was apparent from the earliest days of campaigning for the New Hampshire primary, the first serious test of presidential contenders in 1992. Candidates tramped through the snow to meeting halls across the state, where voters asked specific questions and expected specific responses. The popularity of an eighty-six-page booklet by former senator Paul Tsongas, a Democratic hopeful from neighboring Massachusetts, symbolized the hunger of many for substance instead of slogans. Titled "A Call to Economic Arms," the document was a sobering examination of the economy and the ballooning federal debt, with definite proposals to deal with the problems. Other candidates distributed less elaborate but detail-oriented publications or thirty-minute videotapes discussing the issues. The brief sound-bite or paid spot, so popular in 1988, took a backseat to these more expanded modes of communication. And from all of the reporting from New Hampshire it was easy to see an engaged and active electorate. When Gennifer Flowers ceremoniously confessed that she'd had an affair with Clinton, eyebrows raised but didn't stay there very long. There was a similar reaction to stories that Clinton cleverly avoided the draft as a college student.

Four days before the primary on February 18, *The New York Times* reported, "Throughout the day, the voters asked Mr. Clinton about Medicare, AIDS, the deficit and the future of the Haitian refugees; but the reporters who swarmed around him at every stop asked about the draft." Granted, journalists are more inclined to pose personal questions to a public figure; but what was emerging in New Hampshire was what later could be recognized as a two-track campaign. Insiders within the political community—politicians, consultants, pollsters, pundits—shared a particular perspective (such as Clinton's character questions were fatally crippling or Perot's support was shaky and shallow), while those removed from the inner workings of the political process—the people at large—kept talking and acting differently.

In part, of course, the insiders had been conditioned by past experience (Gary Hart's demise prior to the 1988 election and John Anderson's dismal showing in 1980), but more significant was the public's willingness to look beyond, or at least around, the political elite to make judgments for themselves about the candidates and their messages. Insiders seemed to be getting in the way and not paying close enough attention to the anger, fear, and alienation across the land. By the last few weeks of the fall campaign, with huge audiences gathering for the debates, talk shows, and infomercials, it had become stunningly clear that the people wanted to decide their choice for president based on what *they*, rather than others, considered important. Although the campaign had two tracks for several months, at the end the train engineered by the collective force of the citizens was the only one that really mattered. Insiders were off to the side, shaking their heads and wondering if they would ever regain the power and influence that they thought they had once enjoyed.

No one could have predicted the two-track campaign; however, from watching the media coverage a comparison to a roller-coaster ride might be more apt to describe what happened. Never before had so many different sources of communication provided their "take" on candidates competing for the presidency. The cover of the January 27, 1992 issue of *Time* asked in large type: "Is Bill Clinton for Real?" and went on to say: "Why both hype and substance have made him the Democrats' rising star." The front page of the tabloid *Star* for January 28, 1992 shrieked "Sex Scandal Rocks Race for White House: Ex-aide charges in court Dems' Front-Runner Bill Clinton Cheated With Miss America and four other beauties—a former Miss Arkansas, a singer, a reporter and his own press spokeswoman." Having these two publications vying for attention at the same time—and almost a month before the New Hampshire primary—foreshadowed the disparate types of messages that would bombard the public for the next several months.

Journalists at mainstream news sources—major newspapers, wire services, weekly newsmagazines, and broadcast networks—planned different approaches for 1992 to avoid the mistakes and manipulation that took place in 1988. In *Covering the Presidential Primaries*, a report of The Freedom Forum Media Studies Center, seven "Lessons of 1988" reflected the media's awareness of earlier problems and implied changes would occur this time:

1. *The Horse Race*. The press, the argument goes, devoted too much attention to the political process and the question of who's on top to the exclusion of other critical aspects of the campaign.

2. *Meaningless Photo Opportunities*. The press allowed itself to fall victim to handlers who put their candidates outside a flag factory or inside a tank.

3. *Issues*. The press did not provide sufficient analysis of candidate positions on the major issues of the campaign.

4. *Advertising*. Given the importance of candidate advertising as a source of information for voters, the press failed to give it adequate scrutiny and to refute claims that were patently false.

5. *Voters*. The focus on the horse race and a heavy reliance on political pundits left voters and their concerns out of the picture.

6. *Character*. The press paid too much attention to the scandalous details and not enough to the more substantive aspects of candidates' backgrounds.

7. *Sound Bites*. Candidate sound bites shrunk to an all-time low of about nine seconds.[2]

To a considerable degree, the media succeeded in downplaying photo opportunities, in amplifying the issues, in analyzing and criticizing the ads, in airing the voters' concerns, and in subordinating the significance of the sound bite. Polls (and stories about the polls) kept the horse race nature of the campaign in front of the public, but with three candidates in serious contention much of the time that's probably to be expected. It was the vast gray and murky area of character that again proved difficult for the media to navigate. With the decline of a candidate screening process by in-the-know party leaders and the rise of tell-all personality journalism, news people in recent years came to the conclusion that they should assume the role of "character cops." Who else could do this?

The assignment of probing a public figure's private life, past and present, has no definite rules, and the vague guidelines that exist about private affairs affecting public performance usually provoke controversy when they're outlined. "Where should the line be drawn?" is frequently asked, but answers vary depending on the specific circumstances. In the absence of an acceptable set of standards, each case presents itself as a dilemma for those defining news. The public, too, gets in the act either by showing interest in the story or by signaling their disapproval of what's being revealed.

The tabloid sensationalism that swirled around Bill Clinton before the New Hampshire primary was the most striking example of the media's character problem. In late January and early February, you couldn't pass by a supermarket checkout line without learning something new about the then-governor of Arkansas. Here are some of the front-page headlines after the first one in the *Star*:

- "My 12-Year Affair With Bill Clinton" (*Star*, February 4, 1992)
- "Gennifer Flowers: I Won't Go to Jail for Bill Clinton" (*Star*, February 11, 1992)
- "Bill Clinton Lied on TV about Affair . . . Reveals Lie Detector" (*National Enquirer*, February 11, 1992)
- "Bill Clinton's Drug Dealing Brother Gets Hush-Hush Job on Designing Women" (*Globe*, February 11, 1992)
- "Bill Clinton's Four-in-a-Bed Sex Orgies with Black Hookers" (*Globe*, February 18, 1992)

Covering political figures was nothing new for the tabloids. Back in 1987, the *National Enquirer* published a picture of Gary Hart with model Donna Rice on his lap, suggesting that all the rumors then circulating about them might well be true. What was different about 1992 was the influence of such highly questionable sources of information on the ostensibly reputable, mainstream media. The *Star* released its "world exclusive interview" with Gennifer Flowers the early afternoon of Thursday, January 23. That evening, ABC's "Nightline," one of the most distinguished programs in broadcasting, focused on the story and the questions it raised. Three nights later, Bill and Hillary Clinton discussed their marriage and its problems before an audience of approximately fifty million on CBS's "60 Minutes." The next day, Gennifer Flowers conducted a free-for-all news conference, arranged by the *Star*, that was carried live by CNN. It was another instance of the media swarming like flies at a road-kill.

What's worth noting about these facts is the interplay between a dubious source—the *Star* had paid Ms. Flowers dearly for the story and the tabloid's hype was clearly intended to spike sales—and respected channels of political communication. The contemporary media environment is so cluttered and innerconnected that it becomes difficult to distinguish among the lower and higher forms whenever a big story hits. In such circumstances, the media become one large echo chamber, and everyone frantically races around to produce the next loud, attention-getting message. Increasingly, for the sake of capturing and holding an audience tempted by a widening array of sources, people in communications treat certain stories with an almost self-defeating fascination. In his book *The Age of Overkill*, published in 1962, Max Lerner described a Cold War world with nuclear weapons able to destroy the planet not once but many times. That type of "overkill" is, to be sure, different from the media's today, but the word is apropos. A citizen frequently finds coverage excessive, as traditional news standards strain under the weight of so many institutions attempting to report something fresh and engaging. Analyzing the trivialization of substance by mainstream, previously respected information providers, David Shaw of *The Los Angeles Times* has noted, "In the process, the media have not only blurred the lines between responsible journalism and sensationalism, they have undermined their own integrity and credibility and—worse—they have given readers and viewers an increasingly distorted picture of their society and of themselves."

Paddy Chayefsky once remarked, "Television is democracy at its ugliest." In the contemporary communications environment and with particular stories (political or otherwise), Chayefsky's observation applies to the media as a whole. Amy Fisher, Lorena and John Bobbitt, the Menendez brothers, Tonya Harding—not to mention Woody Allen or Michael Jackson—come along, and the decision is made to devote time or space to covering what these people have done or what allegedly they have done. If the public seems interested, then the stories receive sustained attention until people finally turn away and "elect" to watch or follow something else. There is, of course, a democratic quality to this experience, but one wonders about leadership and professional responsibility. Fearful of losing or even momentarily dispersing a crowd, the media merely follow it.

Who is in charge? With so many different sources working at such speed it becomes difficult to tell who's really advancing the story—and if, indeed, the story has merit in the first place and deserves to be advanced by additional coverage. In the aftermath of the Gennifer Flowers charges, Everette E. Dennis noted: "While all media have every right to cover the campaign, the more serious press devoted to public affairs did little to tell its readers and viewers how to 'read' and understand tabloid fare from a standpoint of facts, balance and fairness. Instead, tabloid headlines simply became fodder for mainstream coverage. In some instances, the presumably more reliable mainstream press did not even do independent fact-checking when using information from the tabloids, which are notorious for their reliance on psychics and their fictional accounts of celebrities."[3] In his book *Strange Bedfellows* about the media and the 1992 campaign, Tom Rosenstiel says of the *Star* story: "It was a form of Gresham's law: When the number of journalistic outlets has so proliferated and each has access to the same information, the bad journalism drives out the good. Since technology and economics have democratized the information flow, the media are now only as good as the worst member of the press."[4]

Interestingly, however, the mainstream press went through a period of collective self-reflection, if not genuine second-guessing, shortly after the intensity of interest in the *Star* charges flickered out. *The Boston Globe* saw Clinton fighting "the scandal machine," with columnist

Tom Oliphant asserting, "That is why I am rooting like a fanatic for Bill and Hillary Clinton to prevail over a naked attempt by pornographers, learned thumb suckers and go-along hacks to hijack democracy." In *The New York Times*, Howell Raines noted, "The barking on the panel shows and the rise of print and television tabloids have undermined the credibility and muddied the ethics of the 'quality' press."

Such media criticism notwithstanding, George Bush experienced a similar, though lower voltage, questioning of his character months later, when the *New York Post* carried the "shocking story" of what it called in three-inch letters "The Bush Affair." The tabloid devoted almost four pages to an alleged "Swiss Tryst" that reportedly took place in 1984, involving Vice President Bush and an assistant, Jennifer Fitzgerald. The same day the *Post* appeared (August 11, 1992), Bush was asked about the story by a CNN reporter at a news conference and by Stone Phillips of NBC during a White House interview for the evening news magazine "Dateline NBC." Again, a report originating in a source more noted for sensationalism than anything else rapidly found its way to the center of mainstream media attention—and, in this case, less than a week before the opening of the Republican National Convention.

Deciding exactly where to draw the line concerning matters of character continued to be a problem for the media. Making matters worse was the greater reliance of politicians on highly personal stories about themselves to create a stronger emotional connection with the public. Clinton, for example, told about growing up in a household with an abusive, alcoholic stepfather, his mother's cancer, even his daughter's reaction to his confession on "60 Minutes" to "causing pain in my marriage." Such private revelations might humanize a candidate, but it somehow seems unfair to cry foul when the media try to probe behind a consciously created image to see if there might be other personal elements indicating less self-enhancing characteristics.

The media today, in all of their variety and devotion to scrutinizing as much as possible of a politician's life, can't be expected merely to amplify what a public figure wants the citizenry to see or to know. It's a two-way street, with a number of detours and dead ends. The trick, of course, comes in dealing with personal concerns fairly—and understanding that "character" is considerably more than what happens behind a bedroom door. As Larry J. Sabato argues in *Feeding Frenzy*:

> Journalists ought to put more emphasis on *public* character than *private* character. . . . Part of the public side of character is on the record and easily accessible, such as courage demonstrated by taking issue stands that may be unpopular with the public at-large or special interest groups. Other aspects, less frequently commented on, include a finely developed sense of humor or irony, the ability to rebound from setbacks and frustrations, the degree to which a person tends to shade the truth or deny reality, and an individual's general openness or secretiveness. The two most telltale indicators of public character are surprisingly little explored: how the candidate relates to his or her working associates and peers, and how he or she deals with staff.[5]

Greater consideration of a politician's public character would help provide more rounded and telling coverage. As with stories of a more private nature, the public might learn information at variance with the official, campaign-approved biography. Especially in the case of a candidate for high office who quickly emerges from obscurity, it's only natural to ask questions related to character. By restricting the responses to a few areas of private life—one above all, to be sure—it's difficult to see the politician in fuller human dimension.

But an important lesson of 1992 was that a tidal wave of titillating news didn't sink a national candidate. Bill Clinton and everyone else learned that most people were more concerned about their own personal lives—their economic condition, their outlook for employment, their costs for health care—than they were about questions in the personal life of another individual. This isn't to say that the stories about Clinton's possible affairs and later about his efforts to avoid the draft bounced off the public without any impact. It's just that people put other factors and concerns above these matters. Those who voted for Clinton and many who didn't considered the country's present state and future prospect more significant than one person's past.

Looking back at media performance for much of the campaign, Peter Jennings, the ABC News anchor, told *The New York Times*, "While we were all trying to run Bill Clinton to the ground on the subject of Gennifer Flowers, the voters in New Hampshire wanted to know about the economy. And we were getting in their way." As it turned out, what happened in New Hampshire— the involvement of the tabloids and the relative indifference of the citizenry to a sensational, personal story—set the stage for what later occurred. A much wider array of communication sources provided political messages, and voters found ways of demanding the information they considered most relevant to their needs. The intense public interest, first seen in New Hampshire, helped candidates find their own ways of going around the traditional outlets for political news to establish less mediated forms of communication.

Town meetings instead of press conferences, talk shows instead of public affairs programs, and citizen forums instead of journalist-dominated debates broadened the political media environment and reduced the distance between the politician and the potential voter. Even before Ross Perot became a major force—and broadened the political media environment even further—a new phenomenon had been identified that put what was taking shape in a clarifying context. In the March 5, 1992 issue of *Rolling Stone*, Jon Katz, a newspaper editor and network producer turned critic and novelist, explained that a new world of "New News" now existed along with the established, highly traditional realm of "Old News." For some people, the shock of the new was unsettling, but for many others previously closed windows and doors of appraisal and participation came open with satisfying, even salubrious, effect. As barriers came down, political communication broadened and encompassed territory worth exploring. Katz wrote:

> Straight news—the Old News—is pooped, confused and broke. Each Nielsen survey, each circulation report, each quarterly statement, reveals the cultural Darwinism ravaging the news industry. The people watching and reading are aging and dying, and the young no longer take their place. Virtually no major city daily has gained in circulation in recent years (*The Washington Post* is one of the few exceptions). In the last decade, network news has lost nearly half its audience. Advertising revenues are drying up.
>
> In place of the Old News, something dramatic is evolving, a new culture of information, a hybrid New News—dazzling, adolescent, irresponsible, fearless, frightening and powerful. The New News is a heady concoction, part Hollywood film and TV movie, part pop music and pop art, mixed with popular culture and celebrity magazines, tabloid telecasts, cable and home video.

Increasingly, the New News is seizing the functions of mainstream journalism, sparking conversations and setting the country's social and political agenda. It is revolutionizing the way information reaches people and moves among them. It is changing the way Americans evaluate politicians and, shortly, elect them.

Of course, with the "New News," lines between information and entertainment fade even more than before, and trashy news sources (tabloid publications as well as "A Current Affair" or "Hard Copy" on television) compete with more serious journalistic efforts. As messages come from so many different directions, there's the risk of confusing the public as they try to decide who can actually govern as opposed to who's merely an accomplished political actor. Frankly, it's somewhat frightening to read the remark of a supporter of Jerry Brown, who told a wire service reporter before the Michigan primary in March 1992, "When I listen to him it's like listening to Oprah. No bull. Nothing to hide." In his long career, Jerry Brown has tried on as many political identities as Oprah Winfrey has tried out diets. Sometimes the insider politician, sometimes the outsider anti-politician, Brown benefited from well-heeled special interests until 1992, when being the candidate of small contributions became advantageous. The word "chameleon" frequently appears in profiles about Brown. He didn't "hide" his past, but a citizen couldn't learn the whole story by relying on town meetings or call-in programs, the here and now messages.

However, on balance, the "New News" is valuable, with the new forms bringing the public closer to the candidate as he or she might be during a particular campaign. In addition, the quantity of political information increases as public figures discover more avenues to our homes. All these different settings allow the audience-electorate additional angles for viewing and evaluating politicians. Oftentimes questions from the people or host focus on substantive problems of general concern rather than on intrigues of political process or tactical maneuvering within a campaign. Moreover, on the same premise that any reading is better than none, the possibility exists that exposure to non-traditional outlets of political communication will spark interest leading to greater personal probing of the candidates and issues.

Yet, even in this environment of "New News," there's a definite place for "Old News," especially in providing background, context, and verification. Old-fashioned, shoe-leather reporting—about the candidates, their life-histories, their strengths and weaknesses for serving in public office, their voting records, their policy—adds a critical dimension that helps citizens form their opinions and make their judgments. As a result of what happened in 1992, the concept of "being informed" now means one needs to combine what's learned from the "New News" with what can be ascertained from the "Old News." In demanding greater democratization of political information, the people (knowingly or not) are shouldering more responsibility, and the future promises even more potential outlets requiring additional scrutiny.

A principal question about political communication flowing from 1992 is: Will the public's interest continue to be as intense as it was, or will it decline when faced with different and changing circumstances? So many elements converged in this election—the hunger of an angry electorate for answers to their problems, the backlash against the sound-bites and negative spots of 1988, the impact of the "New News" with the proliferation of sources for political information, and the emergence, via talk shows of Ross Perot as a presidential candidate and his later use of "infomercials" on television to spread his message. Clinton, Bush, and Perot appeared ninety-six times on just five talk shows ("CBS This Morning,"

"Donahue," "Good Morning America," "Today," and
"Larry King Live") during the campaign, with Clinton
tallying forty-seven visits, Perot thirty-three, and Bush
sixteen. The most often mentioned opinion leaders of
1992, according to one study, were Larry King, David
Brinkley, David Broder, Arsenio Hall, and George Will.

In his autobiographical account, *On the Line: The
New Road to the White House*, Larry King says,

> There was a revolution in 1992. It happened on
> shows like ours and it grew out of the public's distrust
> of, and disgust with, their poll-driven leaders and their
> perceived coconspirators in the traditional press. The
> 1992 campaign marked an adjustment in America's
> low-calorie sound-bite diet. Deficits, taxes, recession,
> and scandal turned once-complacent voters—and
> nonvoters—angry with politics and the wasteful, inept
> government it produced. Moreover, the public saw
> the traditional press as snide, frenzy-driven trivializers
> who were contributing to the erosion of their democ-
> racy. Waning confidence in the media rivaled the
> public's anger at Washington.[6]

But in future years will a Larry King or an Arsenio
Hall be as inviting to politicians and as influential with
the public if there isn't as much interest in an election
as there was in 1992? If sources of the "New News"
become fickle and decide to do less politically, where
does that put the people?

Bill Clinton and Ross Perot adapted to—and even ex-
ploited—the changing political media environment.
George Bush always seemed out of place and ill at ease as
he tried to campaign in this new, less-filtered climate of
citizen interest and participation. The sources of popular

communications, by emphasizing sound bites, negative ads, and photo opportunities, might have worked to Bush's advantage in 1988, but 1992 was markedly different. No longer seen as an ally, the media became an enemy. The only memorable bumper sticker read: "Annoy the Media: Re-elect Bush."

Yet the blame for the wayward course of the campaign was misplaced. In an atmosphere hungry for substance, the media messengers had no Bush message to transmit. As election day drew near, Bush tried to make himself look good by describing Clinton and his vice-presidential running mate Al Gore as "Waffle Man" and "Ozone Man." At one point he told a crowd, "My dog, Millie, knows more about foreign policy than these two bozos. It's crazy." The choice of words was not only unpresidential but in its way pathetic. A career in public service and politics was coming to an end with the figure flailing and railing. This wasn't supposed to have happened.

Throughout 1991, as well-known Democrats with White House aspirations tendered their regrets not to run, the inevitability of Bush winning a second term became an article of faith in the political community. If there was a chance for a Democrat, politicians with the talents and egos of Lloyd Bentsen, Bill Bradley, Mario Cuomo, Richard Gephardt, Al Gore, Jesse Jackson, Sam Nunn, and Jay Rockefeller wouldn't be sitting on the sidelines, would they? Clearly the Democrats were fielding a "B" team of has-beens or will-bes. Jerry Brown, Bill Clinton, Tom Harkin, Bob Kerrey, Paul Tsongas, and Douglas Wilder possessed political skills, but enough for the presidency? Come now.

With no real competition to worry about, Bush and his advisors were slow to take the re-election campaign seriously. When the multi-media pundit Pat Buchanan tossed himself into the Republican race in late 1991, there was more laughter than concern. Maybe the barb-tongued

Buchanan thought some attention in the political arena would result in an expanded speaking schedule with more lucrative fees after the election. As much as anything, Buchanan's candidacy demonstrated once again how fuzzy the line between the media and politics has become in recent years. The revolving door spins on the local, state, and national levels.

To a great degree, the afterglow of the Persian Gulf War was responsible for blinding "A" team Democrats—and Bush himself. When post-war approval ratings soared to an altitude approaching 90 percent in the first half of 1991, the prospect of a difficult re-election bid didn't seem remote but impossible. Later in the year, the Soviet Union ceased to exist, and the Cold War officially came to an end. America had prevailed internationally, diminishing threats from the outside. On the world stage, where Bush most enjoyed performing as president, the United States occupied a commanding place. But victories abroad turned the attention of Americans inward, to home and to the domestic problems so troubling to growing numbers of citizens.

With no foreign adversary to speak of or to fear, the public—and the media—could now focus on the economy and its many aspects—employment, heath care costs, the government's budget deficit and debt, foreign trade—as well as social concerns, such as education, crime, drugs, race relations, homelessness, and the environment. Looking homeward was a natural phenomenon for the nation; however, it put Bush at a disadvantage. He not only showed little interest for domestic affairs, but (as commentator Mark Shields wisely noted a number of times) Bush's great success in winning the Persian Gulf War became a yardstick for the people to use in measuring whatever else he did—or didn't do. The military victory had been prudently planned and swiftly executed. Why couldn't he take charge at home so decisively?

One answer, of course, is that a president has greater latitude for direct action internationally. Congress is a major player in foreign affairs; yet as long as a president is leading in a way that's generally approved, members of the Senate and House are inclined to support an administration's initiatives, especially if what's proposed won't cost too much or take too long. Domestically, however, it's another story. In this sphere, there are ramifications in every state and congressional district. The truism of all politics being local takes on greater meaning, and the potential of divisiveness becomes much more pronounced. Bush himself knew these dynamics, and personally tried to avoid the battles an active domestic agenda would bring. Another significant factor was Bush's own political preference or psyche. As *Newsweek* reported in its special election issue, "The world was Bush's oyster. Mention domestic policy, one pal said, and his eyes would glaze over; his people learned not to schedule meetings on the subject later than, say, 2:30 or 3, when there were always excuses for him to play hooky."

But Bush should have known better. In the September 17, 1990 issue of *U.S. News & World Report*, a major story focused on "Bush's Split Personality: He loves the motion and intrigue of foreign affairs, but is in a slump on domestic matters." A few months later and with characteristic fanfare, *Time* named "The Two George Bushes" as "Men of the Year." The lead article of the January 7, 1991 edition carried the headline: "A Tale of Two Bushes: One finds a vision on the global stage; the other still displays none at home." Over a year before embarking on his re-election campaign, Bush and his aides were well aware of the greatest vulnerability. Yet there was no concerted effort either to achieve anything or even to create the perception of doing something.

Since running for president in 1988, Bush had made fun of his difficulty with "the vision thing," what he saw as his inability to articulate an agenda or program in stirring rhetoric. The phrase, however, was much less of a laughing matter over time as it became conspicuously apparent that a deficiency of oratorical skill was only one aspect of the problem. More fundamental was the absence of a conceptual framework, a vision itself, to animate and direct domestic policy. In his novel *Rabbit at Rest*, John Updike describes the perceptions of Harry (Rabbit) Angstrom about Ronald Reagan and George Bush. According to Updike, Rabbit missed "Reagan a bit, at least he was dignified, and had that dream distance; the powerful thing about him as President was that you never knew how much he knew, nothing or everything, he was like God that way, you had to do a lot of it yourself. With this new one [Bush] you know he knows something, but it seems a small thing."[7] The truth of this fiction rang true with more and more people in late 1991 and into 1992.

Although Bush had served eight years as Reagan's loyal vice president, the two men's presidential styles couldn't have been more different. Unlike Reagan who had vision in abundance and an actor's gift to dramatize his ideas, Bush preferred dealing with matters that crossed his desk and that could be resolved internally within the government. As assessments of Reagan continue to appear, the "Great Communicator" receives criticism for stressing the "bully pulpit" aspect of presidential leadership at the expense of more vigilant governmental administration. Accounts by former Reagan assistants and by others (most notably Lou Cannon in *President Reagan: The Role of a Lifetime*) portray a figure engaged in inspiring people and promoting programs, but bored to the point of slumber with the details of governance. Everything might have looked great from the outside, but who was watching the government?

By contrast, Bush adopted a hands-on, personal style, devoid as much as possible of political theatre. The telephone replaced the television camera as the preferred instrument of communication. Throughout his administration, Bush seemed tone-deaf to the inspirational potential of rhetoric and image-blind to the significance of symbolic pictures. It was as though, in a desire to be his own man, Bush sought to be distinctly different from his popular predecessor. Behind-the-scenes action dominated, but who could watch? And what was he really doing, if there was no strategic vision or definite program?

A major failure for Bush was a lack of reasoned balance—not merely between international and domestic affairs but also more significantly between attention-to-detail statecraft and attention-arresting stagecraft. Not maintaining the appropriate balance comes at a price, in the political short term and the historical long term. Bush, who stressed his type of statecraft, discovered this on election day, when he received the lowest percentage of votes (37.45 percent) for an incumbent president since William Howard Taft won 23.2 percent in his failed re-election bid of 1912. Reagan's undue emphasis on stagecraft had begun to take its toll, too, once people retrospectively were able to look behind the scenes and learn just how "produced" that presidency had been. Public approval of Reagan markedly declined after he left office—Jimmy Carter fared better in most opinion surveys about former presidents—and evaluations by experts questioned much that had been allowed to happen between 1981 and 1989. The Iran-Contra affair, which dogged Bush's steps in his campaigns of 1988 and 1992, was one of several illegal and venal undertakings on Reagan's watch that we are supposed to believe missed presidential notice.

Despite eight years as vice-presidential understudy, it probably would have been too much to expect George Bush to be someone other than himself. Having an ideology that helps create a vision was never important to

Bush, who valued public service above all else. (Presidential history would have turned out quite differently if Jimmy Carter had retained Bush as director of the Central Intelligence Agency during Carter's term. Bush wanted to stay in the post that would have kept him out of presidential politics in 1980, but Carter declined.) Along with public service, Bush prized direct personal relations over indirect public relations mediated by the different forms of popular communications.

In his sprawling yet absorbing book, *What It Takes*, Richard Ben Cramer traces the lives of six men who ran for president in 1988. His portrait of Bush reveals a public figure never interested in thinking through a coherent, consistent political plan let alone a more encompassing philosophy. In 1964, when Bush decided to get into politics by running for the Senate from Texas, he found Barry Goldwater's ideological presidential campaign to be just fine with him. As Cramer writes, "Tell the truth, Bush's program wasn't in conflict with Goldwater's . . . as Bush didn't have a program. Sure, he was conservative—a businessman who had to meet a payroll—but that's about as far as it went, on policy." In the next paragraph, Cramer continues, "Tell the truth, Bush wasn't much for programs, one way or the other. It wasn't that he wanted to do anything . . . except a good job. He wanted to *be* a Senator."[8] Twenty-three years later in 1987, when Bush as vice president decided to seek the presidency, nothing had really changed: "The fact was, he wanted to *be* President. He didn't want to be President to *do* this or that. He'd do . . . what was *sound*."[9]

Winning in 1988 gave Bush his chance "to *be* President," but occupying the White House just reinforced his commitment to a vague sense of public service. In the August 3, 1992 issue of *Newsweek*, Joe Klein noted in a column that Bush's "lack of conviction is manifest. Even Bush allies emerge from the Oval Office shaking their heads over his lack of purpose. 'I asked about his plans for a second term,' says one. He said, 'I'll handle whatever comes up. . . .'" Bush never gave potential voters a reason—or set of reasons—to re-elect him. Unlike 1988, when he could run as the legitimate heir of a then-popular president and within a campaign climate that let him negatively define his opponent, Bush in 1992 had to articulate exactly why he should continue to serve the public. It wasn't in him—and his vast network of friends wasn't of much value.

Presidential leadership requires knowing what direction to take the nation and having the ability to persuade people you'll never meet or know why the particular course is appropriate. In the changing political media environment that stresses using the many forms of popular communication, Bush was unable to rely on his self-established support group. In *What It Takes*, Cramer captures the complexity of Bush's compulsion for "friends," with 30,000 of them included on his private Christmas card list:

> The funny thing was, everybody heard Bush use that word, "friend," a hundred times a day, but they never could see what it meant to him.
>
> By what extravagance of need and will did a man try to make thirty thousand friends?
>
> By what steely discipline did he strive to keep them—with notes, cards, letters, gifts, invitations, visits, calls, and silent kindnesses, hundreds every week, every one demanding some measure of his energy and attention?
>
> And by what catholicity (or absence) of taste could he think well of every one of them?
>
> He could not.
>
> But they would never know that.

The funny thing was, the friendship depended not on what Bush thought of them, but what they thought of him, or what he wanted them to think. If they thought well of him, then, they were friends.[10]

With neither a program nor direction, leadership can become hollow, a void friends and acquaintances can't fill. For Bush, the absence of animating ideas let alone a political philosophy made him see his world in personal terms. People were either with him or against him. When they were against him and also threatening him, then spine and purpose were directed against personalized opponents. Michael Dukakis—and the country—found out Bush was not a wimp in 1988. Manuel Noriega and Saddam Hussein later learned what could happen if Bush perceived someone as his enemy. There was every expectation that Bush would deal with Clinton with bare-knuckle rhetoric, but in 1992 the approach didn't work.

Bush framed the election as a decision about "trust" and "character," two traits of a personal nature to be sure. Clinton presented the view that citizens should consider "change" as the most important factor. Change won. Bush and those working for him kept their sights set on Clinton directly. In the spirited debate among vice-presidential candidates in 1992, Dan Quayle used the word "truth" fifteen times and frequently repeated the phrase "to pull a Clinton" in an effort to raise doubts. Mary Matalin, the Bush campaign's political director, told a journalist in a widely reported exchange about Clinton, "We've never said to the press that he's a philandering, pot-smoking, draft dodger." The reporter responded, "The way you just did?" To which Matalin answered, "The way I just did." That this little duet received so much attention illustrates the game insiders play. News people become willing participants, especially if an element of conflict elbows its way into the story. The more vivid the quotation, the greater the chance of prominent usage.

But in the angry and anxious atmosphere of 1992, the people didn't want candidates to dwell on negative, personal attacks. In talk show after talk show as well as during the second presidential debate that featured citizen participation, the refrain of "What will you do?" reverberated. Although intensely competitive, Bush was playing on a field foreign to him, and it seemed that whatever he tried failed. As mentioned earlier, Bush and his allies charged the media with bias throughout the fall campaign, but an important reason the coverage seemed so negative was that it merely reflected a campaign lacking the necessary substance and full of disarray. When Perot re-entered the race on October 1, the situation became even more complicated because the Bush campaign couldn't direct all its fire at one opponent.

Other factors, too, played a part in the defeat. An old saw says that history doesn't repeat itself, but it often rhymes. Throughout 1992, Bush was haunted by comparisons to Martin Van Buren, the eighth president and the last sitting vice president before Bush to win the White House. Van Buren, however, was unsuccessful in his re-election campaign of 1840, and the reasons for his defeat struck twentieth-century observers as eerily similar to the circumstances and problems that bedeviled Bush in his effort.

The parallels between Van Buren and Bush begin with their respective predecessors: Andrew Jackson and Ronald Reagan. Both Jackson and Reagan were controversial yet popular two-term presidents who possessed definite political views and that indefinable political commodity called charisma. The power of their personalities helped sustain their followings. Although Jackson was a devout Democrat and Reagan robustly Republican, both shared deep suspicion about government power. The motto of the leading Jacksonian newspaper, the *Washington Globe*, was, "That government is best which governs least." A principal refrain of the Reagan era, first enunciated in the 1981 inaugural speech, was: "Government is not the solution to our problem. Government is the problem."

Both Jackson and Reagan positioned themselves as outsiders taking on Washington, the agents of change tackling the encrusted and unrepresentative status quo. Doers rather than thinkers, Jackson and Reagan are now remembered less for specific deeds than for creating new political climates in the United States. Optimism and nationalistic pride marked the years Jackson and Reagan occupied the White House, and the good feelings about Jackson and Reagan—a residual coattail effect you might call it—played a part in their vice presidents winning their own campaigns. Interestingly, both Van Buren and Bush brought extensive, political-governmental resumés to the presidency.

While living in New York, his native state, Van Buren served as a state senator, attorney general, U.S. senator and governor. He was Jackson's campaign manager before being appointed secretary of state and, later, the vice-presidential running mate. Bush's varied experience included being a member of Congress, United Nations ambassador, chairman of the Republican party, U.S. representative to China, director of the Central Intelligence Agency, as well as the eight years as vice president.

Though a self-made man via success as a lawyer, Van Buren was perceived by many as elitist and aristocratic, aloof from the common folk Jackson celebrated in speeches and cultivated for elections. A consummate insider, Van Buren in his 1836 campaign offered continuity instead of change. One commentator noted that Van Buren "was not regarded as a candidate with vision." He even vowed in his inaugural address to "tread in the footsteps" of Jackson. Bush, too, was widely regarded as an insider with political connections throughout Washington and elsewhere. His membership in the moneyed class was well known, and incidents like his apparent ignorance about how supermarket scanners operated in February 1992 reinforced the impression of someone out of touch with concerns of middle-class working people and the poor. In marked contrast to Reagan's inspirational geniality, Bush had trouble connecting with the American people.

The individual parallels between the uncharismatic duo of Van Buren and Bush just begin the historical comparisons. They are overshadowed by the circumstantial similarities that obtrude themselves between their years as chief executive. In both cases, actions of the popular previous presidents had consequences jeopardizing the political appeal and popularity of their protégés. Jackson's handling of banking and monetary affairs received cheers from the citizenry and projected him as defender of the commoner. He declared war against the Bank of the United States, which was chartered by the federal government and had exclusive right to hold the government's deposits. Jackson objected to the concentrated power of the Bank, saying: "The Bank is trying to kill me, but I will kill it."

Which, in effect, he did. Though criticized for being an undemocratic, elitist institution, the Bank had helped stabilize the economy and protected the nation against rampant speculation. In 1832, when the Bank still regulated the country's money supply, the government made $2.6 million from the sale of public land. By 1836, with Jackson's battle against the Bank over and his presidency near its end, land sales reached $24.9 million. One his-

torian calls this period "an orgy of spending and specu-
lating. . . . Never had the nation seemed so prosperous."

However, the boom went bust shortly after Van Buren
succeeded Jackson. A bank panic in the spring of 1837
resulted in over six-hundred bank failures in the next
few months. Hundreds of other businesses closed their
doors, and the unemployment rate soared. The hard
times of the most serious depression the nation had thus
far experienced made Van Buren vulnerable in his re-
election campaign of 1840. The Whigs, a loose coalition
of anti-Jacksonians, ran William Henry Harrison against
Van Buren. Although a man of wealth with a large
house, Harrison was presented as a simple frontier
farmer. His symbol was a log cabin, and that symbol
along with the slogans of "Tippecanoe and Tyler too!"
and "Van, Van, is a used-up man" substituted for any
platform. Harrison won, using tactics first pioneered by
Jackson. A lesson here, of course, is that "spin" doctors
have long been around American politics, making and
massaging perceptions.

As Van Buren received blame for economic problems
while he served as president, so too did Bush. Troubled
times—complete with business failures, bankruptcies,
unemployment, and sagging consumer confidence—
followed the spending and speculation spree of the
1980s. Economic and political analysts argued over the
causes of the ills plaguing the economy. But Reagan
Administration policies favoring deregulation and tax
advantages for businesses (at the expense of individuals)
are often cited as factors in what happened. In *America:
What Went Wrong?* Barlett and Steele document how
people in business used deductions for interest and
operating losses to avoid taxes and to promote takeovers
and mergers. The savings and loan industry mess, the
"junk bond" excesses, and the mounting federal debt are
also some legacies of the 1980s. The boom-and-bust

cycle recurred—with Bush ultimately paying a political price comparable to the one Van Buren paid.

Besides the curse of Martin Van Buren, larger historical forces were at work in 1992 that Bush couldn't tame or command. Arthur M. Schlesinger, Jr., has inherited from his father the hypothesis that there are cycles of American political history that alternate between periods of private interest or action and times of public interest or action. Each phase recurs approximately every fifteen years, meaning a full cycle of thirty years or roughly a generation.[11] In the November 16, 1992 issue of *The New Yorker*, Schlesinger interpreted Clinton's win as further evidence of the hypothesis. The swing to emphasis on private action that began in the late 1970s under Jimmy Carter and continued in more pronounced fashion under Reagan and Bush had ended with the election of an activist, public-motivated president. In Schlesinger's words, "And so the dialectic of democracy carries the republic into the future, each phase correcting the excesses of the phase before, each phase essential to the equilibrium of the system."

In a number of different ways, 1992 proved George Bush was yesterday's man, a figure who didn't understand the implications of the changing political media environment or the need to adapt to a particular time that had serious questions about the nation's future. Devotion to "public service" and reliance on "friends" weren't enough for the electorate to reward him with another four years in the White House.

On election night 1992, shortly after Ross Perot conceded the presidential race, a reporter shouted a question at the independent candidate who'd just won almost twenty million votes, 18.91 percent of the total cast. "Mr. Perot, Mr. Perot, did you cost George Bush the election?"

Without hesitating, Perot shot back, "No. Did you?" On the evening that signaled the end of Bush's political career, the feisty Perot continued jousting with the press. Given the bizarre circumstances surrounding his candidacy, he probably had good cause. He'd done much better than expected—analysts had predicted that somebody on the ballot without a chance of winning would be lucky to receive 10 percent—and he'd begun building a foundation for the future.

With the decline of the political parties in selecting candidates along with the rise of the media in presenting possible nominees, a public figure's personality takes on increasing significance in American political life. In certain respects, Perot's performance symbolized personality politics in its purest form. An engaging individual effectively presented himself to the public by using different means of communication (particularly the premier medium of personality, television).

A poll conducted in March 1992 reported that over half of the respondents had never heard of Perot. Three months later, 99 percent could identify him—and several other surveys showed him leading both Bush and Clinton as the preferred presidential choice. Perot's rapid ascent reflected the velocity of communication in today's political media environment as well as the volatility—some might say vagary—of opinion formation. In the spring of 1992, a political firestorm was taking place across America, and each of Perot's television appearances produced oxygen for the flames.

Perot's emergence as a serious player in presidential politics resulted from a convergence of forces. The anger and alienation of the people made them distrustful of politics-as-usual and desirous of an alternative from the outside. Perot, a billionaire businessman, was perceived as a take-charge, can-do outsider, who understood the frustration and discontent of the people. Moreover,

Perot's personality was well suited to the talk-show format popular on television, while his wealth allowed him easy access to advertising appeals and other communication messages. The mood, man, media, and money made a movement.

On February 20, 1992, Perot told Larry King and his CNN audience that he would become a presidential candidate if citizens placed his name on the ballots in all fifty states. From that moment on—first without much news coverage and later with a massive amount—Perot became the unknown variable of the 1992 campaign. He gained support so quickly because of what he said and also what he represented. In appearance after appearance, he'd say: "We own this country. Government should come from us. In plain Texas talk, it's time to take out the trash and clean out the barn." Perot's appeal was directly to the people in a folksy manner that seemed both genuine and sincere. He was speaking truth about power—the debilitating government debt affecting the entire economy, the paralyzing gridlock between Congress and the White House that didn't solve problems, the unedifying state of political campaigning that featured distracting sideshows instead of debates about issues. The distemper of the time found a voice.

But there was more to this messenger than just a message of discontent. He framed what he said about the present in the broader context of deeply rooted core beliefs about America. He talked about cultivating rugged individualism, striving for the American dream, making the melting pot work, and returning to town-meeting democracy. Ideals captured in Norman Rockwell paintings, Frank Capra movies, and Fourth of July oratory have a mythic resonance of continuing consequence. What Lincoln called the "mystic chords of memory" still exert a hold among vast numbers of citizens, and Perot struck these chords effectively. Tough-minded political realists found such elements hokey and hopelessly old-fashioned, but they misread their importance and Perot's skill in using them. Perot frequently said he was "a myth, not a legend." His own "myth," if you will, as well as the others he rhetorically embraced merged in a way that offered hope and optimism to many who longed to have America a more unified, less troubled nation. The past, however imagined or romanticized, would help guide people through the stormy present and into a more promising future.

To a certain extent, Perot's appeal was similar to Ronald Reagan's. Both figures used traditional national values to anchor their messages. They seemed strong and commanding, natural for leadership. They spoke in a direct, understandable, engaging manner. They based what they said on common "horse" sense rather than any intellectual theory or approach. They presented themselves as "citizen-politicians," outsiders who for the good of the country were involved in public life because of the failures of professional politicians. They possessed sunny self-assurance and confidence about America's future, particularly the strength of the people to accomplish great things. Above all, they simplified complexities by making perplexing problems easily manageable through use of well-turned phrases that effortlessly dealt with knotty reality. In the mind's eye, both figures were Western men on horseback ready to ride into town (in this case the modern metropolis of Washington) to clean up the place and to set things right.

Watching Perot's supporters during the spring of 1992 was a lesson in grassroots politics in a high-tech era. Sparked by television appearances broadcast nationally, people in the fifty states set to work to get Perot's name on all the ballots. Estimates varied, but somewhere around 350,000 citizens became personally involved in the effort—setting up petition-signing tables, conducting meetings, holding bakesales, and numerous other activities. Sincerity marked the work of these "volunteers," as they tried to do some things themselves to change the country's direction.

In early June, political scientist Theodore J. Lowi called the Perot phenomenon "the radicalization of the middle," and it was certainly that. Ordinary Americans concerned about the present and frightened about the future were taking matters into their own hands in an attempt to have more connection with political life. Modern communications linked many like-minded campaign workers across the country, with procedures and information quickly traded; but the vast number of those involved pitched in to do the hour-consuming, pedestrian jobs required to form an organization. These Perot supporters were motivated by what they saw as a distinctive alternative to status quo politics and governance. At the beginning, too, the media found the euphoria of the movement and the fascination with Perot's personality to be a running "gee whiz" story.

And who could actually argue with much that Perot was saying? In an interview with *Time* (May 25, 1992), he noted, ". . . I have never been around a process that is more irrelevant to the desired end result than this. The process we have for selecting a President is irrelevant to getting a good President for the people. What we have now is mud wrestling and dirty tricks and Willie Horton, and just stuff that everybody goes into a feeding frenzy over. It encourages virtually everybody who might be a good President not to run." Just before this statement in the interview he said, "What is happening has nothing to do with me." In many respects, Perot was right. A presidential campaign in America is a time to take stock of the country and its state as a democracy. So many people now found the process so alienating and government so remote that an independent outsider—selflessly working on their behalf, as he vowed—amassed an immediate following. The intensity of interest in Perot reflected deeper feelings about traditional, two-party politics and the United States in 1992.

The bandwagon, however, began to lose speed in mid-June when Republicans started attacking Perot and the media weighed in with reports scrutinizing the Texan's business practices and prior political activities. Vice President Dan Quayle referred to Perot as a "temperamental tycoon who has contempt for the Constitution of the United States." Several news organizations carried investigative pieces questioning exactly how the Perot billions had been made. Were we really getting what we saw?

The more the public learned about Perot the more paradoxical he seemed. A man of wealth (derived in large part from government contracts) was presenting himself as the populist champion of the average American, disgusted with the government. An autocratic executive used to operating in a closed, secretive way was promoting "town-hall democracy" on a national scale, with the people directing their leaders about what to do. The anti-image ("What you see is what you get") individual who called himself "the servant of the people" was widely known to work hard at cultivating a specific image with a chief characteristic of his own identity the belief in his power to command others. The anti-sound bite, anti-media public figure used both sound bites and the media in general with more skill than many professional performers—or communications savvy politicians.

Besides the paradoxes that raised doubts, there was discussion in the press and among people phoning talk shows that Perot possessed troubling traits more natural to a dictator than to a let-the-people-decide democrat. Perot's height—or lack thereof—contributed to this commentary, and the phrase "Napoleonic complex" started to be seen and heard. Michael R. Beschloss, the historian and president-watcher, noted in a *New York Times* interview: "The record has been that short people who run for President are at a disadvantage when they do demonstrate qualities of great strength and fierceness and determination, because it's very easy to make the leap and assume they have a Napoleonic complex." But Beschloss went on to explain why there was some reason to see Perot in relation to the term: "He has an arbitrariness and an instinctive ability to act on the basis of his own will after consulting a wide array of people. He has a tendency to have excessive faith in his own powers of judgment. He's an iconoclast to the point where he doesn't take advice terribly well."

Millions of Americans, however, were willing to look beyond (or over) such statements and others without any reference to physical stature because they were desperate for someone to solve the problems they saw around them everyday. Perot was prescribing bitter medicine to cure the deficit-debt disease, but at least he was willing to talk about it. Was he dictatorial or tyrannical? Well, let's make that decision later. Back in 1961 in an article for *Life*, Gore Vidal wrote:

> I have often thought and written that if the United States were ever to have a Caesar, a true subverter of the state, (1) he would attract to himself all the true believers, the extremists, the hot-eyed custodians of the Truth; (2) he would oversimplify some difficult but vital issue, putting himself on the side of the majority, as Huey Long did when he proclaimed every man a king and proposed to divvy up the wealth; (3) he would not in the least resemble the folk idea of a dictator. He would not be a hysteric like Hitler. Rather, he would be just plain folks, a regular guy,

warm and sincere, and while he was amusing us on television storm troopers would gather in the streets.[12]

The difference in 1992 was that ordinary, average Americans were largely responsible for the Perot movement. They had become politically active out of frustration. How long they would have been able to bottle up their political emotions before doing something is a matter to wonder about. Personal weaknesses notwithstanding, Perot served as a magnet for the disaffected.

In a speech he gave July 2 which *The New York Times* printed, Perot said, "We can make this country anything we want it to be because of a very special, magic dream. It belongs to you and me. Everybody's worried about me getting sick and tired of all the stuff that gets thrown at you in a political campaign. As far as I'm concerned, those are little insignificant spitballs—they have no impact at all. The only thing that matters to me is what the American people want." Two weeks later, on the day Bill Clinton delivered his acceptance speech at the Democratic National Convention, Perot withdrew from the presidential campaign. "Now that the Democratic Party has revitalized itself, I have concluded that we cannot win in November and that the election will be decided in the House of Representatives," he said, adding that "our program" would "be disruptive to the country." *Newsweek*, which had run a "President Perot?" cover in mid-June, devoted its July 27 cover to "The Quitter," a word that others in journalism also used frequently. The admirer of the Founding Fathers had turned into a Benedict Arnold in the eyes of many of his followers. The "little insignificant spitballs" of criticism did more damage than the recipient cared to admit.

When Perot returned to the race on October 1, there were as many snickers as cheers. His message continued to have merit, but the messenger seemed meretricious. Was this a rich man's ego trip, an effort to remove the label of "quitter" from the public mind, or something else? How sincere did he deserve to be taken? Doubts and all, Perot changed the dynamics of the campaign's last month. Through effective use of thirty-minute "infomercials," three credible debate performances, and other activities, he was able to flip-flop the perception people had of him. A September survey reported 43 percent having a negative opinion of him, with 24 percent positive. A month later, 47 percent viewed him positively and 25 negatively. Before the debates, Perot's support stood at 7 percent; afterwards it measured 21 percent.

Perot's stay in the nation's dog house was short because much that he said still resonated with millions of citizens, and he said it so colorfully. He was willing to spend approximately $60 million of his own money to discuss subjects like the national debt and insider influence in politics that Bush and Clinton preferred to avoid. In the end, he would be seen as the leading actor in the principal subplot of the 1992 political drama. This adroit illusionist gave hope to the disillusioned. His humor—one of his television productions had the memorable title "Deep Voodoo, Chicken Feathers and the American Dream"—tempered the hostility. In addition, he opened the channels of communication by going on the television talk shows, and these appearances as well as the "infomercials" helped expand the availability of political information. The super salesman was selling himself, but there was greater substance for the public to consider as a result of his involvement. His electoral showing was both a reward and a warning. An independent, with a multitude of human imperfections and untraditional techniques, could be competitive given the right circumstances.

Perot's total vote revealed a base of political dissatisfaction that could be of election-deciding significance in the future. A week before Bill Clinton's inauguration January 20, 1993, Perot launched a national membership drive for his political-governmental watchdog group, United We Stand, America. He continued his television appearances and started criss-crossing the country to speak at rallies. According to one reporter who covered Perot, these talks of more than an hour "fan the fires, but he never says how he could take the energy of that fire and put it to use." As he did so skillfully in the campaign, Perot emphasizes what's wrong with Washington and what's right with "the people" while keeping precise solutions to problems troublingly vague. John White, who wrote much of Perot's economic plan for the campaign, said in October 1993: "Perot has served a certain value as a kind of national scold on some of this stuff. But over time, it gets to wear a bit thin. At some point, you have to say, 'We understand what you're against, but what is it you're for?'" Perot says he'd "rather have major surgery without anesthesia" than be a presidential candidate in 1996, yet his organization is so much of a one-man band that it's difficult to imagine him on the sidelines if the anti-political, specifically anti-Washington, mood persists.

In word and deed, Perot is as clever as he is surprising. Leaving the race, he complimented the Democratic Party because it "revitalized itself," and he didn't see a chance of winning—only to return several weeks later. In May 1993, he told David Frost in a television interview, "If I could wish for one thing right now in terms of political parties, it would be for the Republicans to get over the funeral, to revitalize themselves and have strong leadership and to have strong, positive, constructive programs. That's starting to happen." But can such a personality with so many resources ever be satisfied with what he perceives as the revitalization of potential rivals? That's highly doubtful.

Perot hurt himself and his reputation as a master communicator on television when he performed so ineffectively during a debate over the North American Free Trade Agreement with Vice President Al Gore on CNN's "Larry King Live" on November 9, 1993. In a high-risk attempt to build support for NAFTA, the White House decided to pit the vice president against the most visible and vocal opponent of the agreement. The strategy worked for the Clinton Administration in helping to build momentum to pass NAFTA and in showing the Perot of this media encounter as mean-spirited and personally insulting rather than good-humored and confident in the merits of his argument. A month later, *U.S. News & World Report* published a survey that found 55 percent of voters having a negative opinion of Perot—compared to 26 percent six months earlier. Just 28 percent of those polled said they would consider voting for him for president.

However, writing Perot's political obituary is premature. If the bug that's infected the body politic in recent years persists and people continue to feel alienated and insecure, Perot—flaws and all—will be there to talk about their fears and to collect their support.

Devoted runner though he might be, Bill Clinton proved that a presidential race isn't really a metaphorical marathon. With the involvement of all of the media, the gauntlet of the primaries and caucuses, and the feverish nature of the fall campaign with high-stake debates, competing for president today is closer to a continuous Ironman Triathlon, where you swim 2.4 miles in the ocean, ride a bike 112 miles, and run a marathon of 26.2 miles. Such an endurance test takes a certain kind of person. As unlikely as it seemed for so long, Clinton prevailed.

Traditional politician personified—he sought public office in Arkansas eight times between 1974 and 1990— Clinton knew the anti-political mood of America in 1992 and tried to do what he could to respond to it. His campaign speeches frequently included references to *America: What Went Wrong?* and *Why Americans Hate Politics*, especially that book's argument about politics becoming a series of "false choices," where "either/or" approaches to problems foster "artificial polarization." Clinton emphasized the value of E. J. Dionne's "both/and" thinking for greater unity and harmony—and less hatred of politics. In speeches, the candidate described himself as "pro-business and pro-labor," "for affirmative action but against quotas," "for economic growth and for protecting the environment," "for legal abortions but also for making abortion as rare as possible." Dionne ended his book by asserting, "A nation that hates politics will not long thrive as a democracy."[13] Clinton agreed, and the five-term Arkansas governor sternly criticized the politics of stalemate, of partisan tactical advantage seeming to be more significant than solving the nation's problems. This said, it would still be a tightrope walk for someone considered a political insider.

Clinton's participation in the centrist Democratic Leadership Council and his artful avoidance of the perception that he was under the influence of liberal organizations or groups created the impression of "a new Democrat," someone different from Michael Dukakis, Walter Mondale, or George McGovern. At a time when the public was calling for change and looking for someone different to lead, Clinton quickly went to the head of the line. And, to be blunt, the challengers in his party never appeared to be serious or realistic presidential contenders. As Clinton strategist James Carville remarked mid-way through the primaries, "We ain't exactly running against giants."

For a couple of months after the New Hampshire primary, Clinton seemed to be running against himself—what else was there besides Gennifer Flowers, keeping out of the draft, and smoking marijuana without inhaling?—and a phantom candidate Democrats were supposed to be hiding in the wings in case Clinton was forced for some reason to leave the race. Although publicly and privately pundits and politicians pronounced his prospects beyond redemption, he persevered and looked for more ways to go around the press and directly to the people.

In two critical respects, Clinton was the beneficiary of what had happened in recent American history. As mentioned earlier, George Bush's popularity following the Persian Gulf War made a number of bigger name Democrats decide to forgo a bid for the presidency. As a result Clinton began his quest for the White House with the best organization and most resources. In addition, there was an "old news" quality to many of the personal charges leveled at him. Journalists had previously dealt with Gary Hart and allegations of extramarital affairs, Dan Quayle and his possible dance around the draft to avoid service during the Vietnam War, and Douglas Ginsberg, who saw a chance to become a Supreme Court Justice evaporate amid accusations of pot smoking. For many citizens, this was *déjà vu*, and it was personal information at a time when they were more interested in a discussion of broader public problems.

Moreover, the media had become sensitive to charges of voyeurism masquerading as "character coverage." Carville colorfully described journalists as "a bunch of drunks who get together . . . and say, 'We are not going to do this again.' Then everybody gets out of detox and, wow, here comes Gennifer Flowers and it was just like a jigger of whiskey for everybody at the bar and everybody's killing each other to get it." The media binges took place, but though raucously intense, they were relatively brief and early enough in the process that they, too, became "old news" by late spring. The controversial *Time* cover (on its April 20 issue) of the eerie negative of an actual head-shot picture of the candidate with the words "Why Voters Don't Trust Clinton" slapped across it marked a low point. However, Clinton kept going and kept talking about the issues. Journalists saw complexity in him, but had difficulty articulating it. Tom Rosenstiel, a reporter for *The Los Angeles Times*, writes perceptively in his book, *Strange Bedfellows*:

> Like many politicians, Bill Clinton is a man of un-finished and contradictory character—scholarly and shallow, outgoing and shy, principled and craven, the mood depending on the motive. He possesses extra-ordinary talent and a fierce thirst for knowledge and insight, but above all approval. One reporter who spent time with him shortly after the incidents in New Hampshire found him one of the most outwardly di-rected people she had ever met—as if he had little inner sense of self at all. He is also a man, friends would say afterwards, who is capable of deceiving himself. In the best profile written of him during the campaign, Clinton told David Shribman of the *Wall Street Journal* that character was "a quest." The choice of words was curiously apt. Character was something to be searched for. Something not held.[14]

In retrospect, the explosive emergence of Ross Perot during May and June helped Clinton. The news spot-light—and, hence, public concern—now focused more directly on the outsider and his possible independent candidacy. Clinton was no longer so much the center of political attention, and questions about his character or trusting him faded into the background. In fact, except for a stock headshot (on June 3) and a small campaign photo that ran together with those of Bush and Perot (on May 31), only one picture of the Arkansas governor appeared on the front page of *The New York Times* from May 7 until June 28. That shot, published June 5, featured the candidate wearing dark glasses and playing his saxophone on "The Arsenio Hall Show." By comparison, during the same period, there were seven notable pictures of Bush and six of Perot on page one of *The Times*. Neither *Time* nor *Newsweek* nor *U.S. News & World Report* devoted a cover to Clinton in May or June. Their issues dated July 20, coinciding with the Democratic Convention, finally brought him back to newsmagazine prominence.

However, while the established, mainstream news media were looking the other way, Clinton was still finding ways of getting his message to the people. In a column for *The New York Times* after the election, consultants James Carville and Paul Begala discussed their strategy for the Clinton campaign: "Demand for political information—especially a specific plan for the economy—was high. When the traditional media were unable or unwilling to give Bill Clinton time to discuss these issues, we turned elsewhere. Televised town-hall meetings, call-in shows and the appearance on 'The Arsenio Hall Show' were all efforts to supply voters with information about Bill Clinton and his plans. It is a matter of some pride that our campaign pioneered the use of pop-culture media. Ross Perot popularized this, but Bill Clinton was there first."

Perot's departure from the presidential campaign also benefited Clinton. Perot's announcement less than twelve hours before Clinton's acceptance speech at the convention gave the public greater reason to watch and listen to the Democratic candidate as well as his vice-presidential running mate Al Gore. The next day Clinton and Gore built on this interest (and bitterness over Perot) by embarking on the first of several bus trips throughout the country. The excursions served the dual purpose of putting the candidates on the ground in personal proximity to large number of voters in key states and of being telegenic events for the local and national media to cover. Clinton, pretty much unknown when he announced his candidacy October 3, 1991, was re-introducing himself with greater success than he had had in winter and early spring.

From the convention until election day, Clinton effectively combined the hand-shaking, back-slapping techniques of the old style politician with the media-savvy communication skills so important today. In fact, during the bus trips and at other times, he was in direct contact with citizens while also being heavily covered by journalists. Such moments became magnified by the media, especially television, making personal, one-on-one meetings a metaphor for a larger thematic message of human, two-way connection. Moreover, in candidate-citizen exchanges and in talk-show settings with the public asking questions, Clinton in manner and facial expression projected sympathy and empathy, reflecting understanding of the people's problems. That he was able to build on this emotional base with specific, detailed plans he as president would implement gave depth to his message and enhanced his appeal. And people quickly learned that the former Rhodes scholar had studied governmental and economic issues with such assiduity the designation of "policy work" seemed apt. Questions elicited multi-point responses with what seemed an unlimited number of statistics to flesh out his proposals.

Clinton brought to the 1992 campaign personal and political characteristics that meshed well with the time and its tumult. Intelligent, self-confident, personable, and articulate, he seemed resourceful as well as resilient. Imposing physically, he projected the image of someone with a sense of command, who could shoulder the weight of the presidency. His youth suggested vigor and a willingness to work on the goals and new direction he talked about. Being married to a successful professional woman was in its way a sign of the new generation coming of age. When so many citizens thought change was essential—an August *New York Times*/CBS News Poll reported a stunning 92 percent of the public responding "yes" to change—belonging to a generation different in age from the one in power proved an asset. A reputation as a Southern moderate committed to domestic concerns helped, too. Everyone realized international affairs and military matters weren't Clinton's strong suit, but they didn't have to be, many people thought, given what had happened in recent years and, most significantly, the ending of the Cold War. Everything taken together, the candidate conformed to a specific period and its exigencies. Success in politics often comes when a person fits the time.

Adding to Clinton's advantage was his single-minded focus on the paramount concern in the public's mind. The now-famous sign in his Little Rock headquarters, "The Economy, Stupid," provided a chastening daily reminder that, despite distractions of one kind or another, the campaign message needed to be both constant and consistent. Since "the economy" encompassed (among other things) jobs, employment readiness (or education), health care, the deficit/debt dilemma, taxes, and foreign trade, Clinton was able to talk at length about fixing things and changing the course. To his advantage, he could keep to his message in the longer formats of the talk shows and town meetings. Four years earlier, in a much different environment, the slogan "Read my lips:

No new taxes," helped give focus to the Bush campaign. But 1992 demanded amplification—albeit within the framework of a strategy to stick to one subject.

Clinton and people working on his behalf were especially successful at dealing with potentially damaging statements from opponents or questions from the media in a rapid fashion that allowed a quick return to the principal message. By reacting swiftly, the negative information didn't have much chance to seed itself in the public mind, and the response usually ran with the charge. The 1988 presidential campaign had taught that a candidate (George Bush) could define an opponent (Michael Dukakis). Clinton and his staff saw to it that such negative definition would not happen to him.

The new, sophisticated communications technology, with its accelerated news cycle, proved to be a Clinton ally. Oftentimes a charge (about Clinton's personal life or an action as governor) was made, responded to, and gone from consideration in a day's time. This phenomenon helps clear the political air when one campaign says something unfounded or without merit about its principal competition. But what about charges or questions that aren't really resolved and deserve more scrutiny? During the campaign, NBC anchor Tom Brokaw told *The New York Times*, "The news cycle has become a 24-hour-a-day thing, and it moves very fast all the time now. What happens is that a fragment of information, true or false, gets sucked into the cycle early in the morning, and once it gets into the cycle its gets whipped around to the point that it has gravitas by the end of the day. And, unfortunately, people are so busy chasing that fragment of information that they treat it as a fact, forgetting about whether it is true or not." And the chase picks up the next day, frequently in pursuit of an altogether different story. Seeing things steadily and whole is increasingly difficult when it often seems that news is

being defined by people with the attention span of a
four-year-old. Interestingly, as was noted earlier, the
media can also go overboard and provide too much
coverage of certain stories. Finding the proper (if not
golden) mean becomes harder in an environment of
rapid delivery and multiple sources, yet for the sake of
public understanding it deserves the effort.

The expansion of political discourse that the public
demanded worked by and large to Clinton's advantage.
Words tumbled out of his mouth with the ease of the
talk-show hosts he was visiting so regularly, and bouts
with hoarseness or laryngitis were the only barriers
blocking the flow. A person traveling with the candidate,
who kept track during appearances, estimated that Clinton uttered 40,000 words on an average day—about as
many words as you find in this book. Even when pro-
voked to anger, he was pointedly forceful in responding.
In a session with voters during the primaries, he told
one questioner obsessed with what he saw as Clinton's
obsessive ambition: "Let me tell you something. If I
were dying of ambition, I wouldn't have stood up here
and put up with all this crap I've put up with for the last
six months. I'm fighting to change this country. . . . And
I'm sick and tired of all these people who don't know
me, know nothing about my life, know nothing about
the battles I've fought, know nothing about the life I've
lived, making snotty-nosed remarks about how I haven't
done anything in my life and it's all driven ambition.
That's bull, and I'm tired of it."

To be sure, on some occasions, he'd dance around
direct questions to cushion the possible injury to himself
and his candidacy. In the "60 Minutes" interview after
the allegations by Gennifer Flowers began to circulate,
Clinton denied her story and then was asked whether he
had ever committed adultery. "I'm not prepared tonight
to say that any married couple should ever discuss that

with anyone but themselves," Clinton responded. But he also added, "I have acknowledged wrongdoing. I have acknowledged causing pain in my marriage. . . . I think most Americans who are watching tonight—they'll know what we're saying; they'll get it and they'll feel we've been more than candid." It seemed like a confession, but on his terms and somewhat removed from the specific case. A few weeks later, when asked about possible drug use in the past, Clinton told the "Fox Morning News": "I said I've never violated the drug laws of our country, and I haven't." Pressed more closely during a debate on WCBS-TV in New York twenty-seven days after the earlier statement, he admitted, "I've never broken any state laws and when I was in England I experimented with marijuana a time or two and I didn't like it. And I didn't inhale and I didn't try it again." The three words "I didn't inhale" were, of course, intended to soften the blow, but they ended up being a running gag line for comedians that actually made matters worse for Clinton. Protecting himself with his words and pleasing everyone with what he said resulted in verbal contortionism that puzzled many. Fortunately for Clinton the public was more concerned with what he was saying about the country's problems and his proposals for the future.

A representative example of Clinton's skill in expressing himself on public matters is the way he handled one of the questions during the second presidential debate. Held October 15 at Richmond, Virginia, this debate featured citizens rather than journalists probing the candidate. An African-American woman wanted to know, "How has the national debt personally affected each of your lives?" Ross Perot answered by saying the debt disrupted his own business and private life because he felt he had "to get involved in this activity" of running for president to do something to help his children, grandchildren, and "future generations." Then George Bush made three false starts that were interrupted by attempts to give his answer more focus before he said, "I'm not sure I get it. Help me with the question and I'll try to answer it." Another restatement of the woman's question brought a response, but the back-and-forth of the exchange—with Bush glancing at his watch at one point—evoked for yet another time the perception of a president who didn't really understand problems facing average Americans. He seemed out of place and eager for the event to end.

By contrast, Clinton moved toward the woman and the audience for his response. It was a question deserving a perception of closeness with the people there—and through television with the people watching at home. He started by saying, "Tell me how it's affected you again. You know people who've lost their jobs and lost their homes." The woman answered yes—meaning Clinton, unlike Bush, had immediately established the right connection to continue:

> Well, I've been governor of a small state for twelve years. I'll tell you how it's affected me. Every year, Congress and the President sign laws that makes us— make us do more things and gives us less money to do it with. I see people in my state, middle-class people, their taxes have gone up in Washington and their services have gone down while the wealthy have gotten tax cuts. I have seen what's happened in this last four years when in my state, when people lose their jobs, there's a good chance I'll know them by their names. When a factory closes I know the people who ran it. When the businesses go bankrupt, I know them. And I've been out here for thirteen months meeting in meetings just like this ever since October with people like you all over America, people that

have lost their jobs, lost their livelihood, lost their health insurance.

What I want you to understand is the national debt is not the only cause of that. It is because America has not invested in its people. It is because we have not grown. It is because we've had twelve years of trickle-down economics. We've gone from first to twelfth in the world in wages. We've had four years where we've produced no private-sector jobs. Most people are working harder for less money than they were making ten years ago. It is because we are in the grip of a failed economic theory. And this decision you're about to make better be about what kind of economic theory you want. Not just people saying I want to go fix it but what are we going to do. What I think we have to do is invest in American jobs, American education, control American health care costs and bring the American people together again.

To be sure, there's a personal element to Clinton's response, but he effectively turns the personal into his public role as governor and his plan to improve the lives of people like the woman-questioner. The body language and spoken message worked together to create the desired impression. In *Mad as Hell: Revolt at the Ballot Box, 1992,* Jack W. Germond and Jules Witcover focus on the handling of this particular question by Bush and Clinton as a defining moment of the campaign. The president seemed unable to understand what was being asked, while his principal challenger wove facts and emotions into a human response appropriate for the circumstances.[15]

Clinton's victory on November 3 was not a landslide, as some news organizations and political analysts claimed. However, his support (43 percent and almost 45 million votes) along with Perot's nearly 19 percent totaled 62 percent, representing a clear rejection of Bush. "It is not so amazing that America has a 46-year-old president," a French commentator observed. "The amazing thing is that the American system can take someone virtually unknown and within a year catapult him to the top. That could never happen in Europe." A principal characteristic of this nation's system today is its emphasis on the individual political personality and how that figure comes across via the different forms of popular communication. Party deliberation and discipline that are so important in European countries take a backseat here to the collective judgments of increasingly independent and ticket-splitting citizens sizing up candidates on their own and largely through the various lenses of the media.

In 1992, Clinton had to deal with searing journalistic scrutiny, especially of his private life. But his larger political message resonated and took hold, particularly in formats where he could present himself and his points over an extended period of time. Election-day polling revealed that the public didn't believe Clinton told the truth about his past; however, an even greater percentage thought that Bush lied about his role in the Iran-Contra affair. With the economy and jobs the overriding concerns, personal matters were of lesser import. They were factors, of course, but not decisive ones for Clinton voters.

Moreover, the story of the Arkansan's emergence and endurance had a moving, romantically American quality to it. As Peter Guber, the chairman of Sony Pictures Entertainment, told *The New York Times*:

> This is a real John Doe goes to Washington. It's Rocky! A classic movie motif. An underdog. Some guy in his mid-forties who went to Oxford and Yale. Wanted to be president. Wanted to be champion. You would have said, "No way, that wouldn't play in Peoria." He kept getting knocked down like Rocky.

He had an Achilles' heel. People counted him out.
But he came back. He became champion. It touched
a chord in some primal way.

Even tabloid attention turned full circle, sort of. A post-
election cover (December 8, 1992) of the *National Enquirer* showed a loving picture of the president-elect
holding the head of his wife, and there was the large
headline: "Hillary Clinton: How I Saved My Marriage."
Underneath the promise of "Intimate secrets of the new
First Lady" appeared another picture, this one of the
Clinton cat Socks and a somewhat smaller headline:
"New White House Cat Faces Nervous Breakdown—
The Untold Story." There was always something to worry
about, it seemed.

In his first news conference following the election,
Clinton noted that "I have to do my best at one of the
most important jobs of a president, which is to communicate to the American people." Recognition of the significance of stagecraft in statecraft is important, but the
public cares more about governmental, programmatic
execution. They wonder: What is the president trying to
communicate, and what does it mean for us? During the
transition and early months of the Clinton Administration, there were a number of skillfully executed occasions featuring the president, notably the economic
conference in Little Rock before taking office, his inaugural speech, his economic address to a joint session of
Congress, his participation in a summit in Tokyo for
leading industrial countries, his highly public trips to visit
flood victims and sites along the Mississippi River, and his
speech to Congress announcing his health care program.
But a lack of consistency and strategic planning in the
president's use of what Theodore Roosevelt referred to
as the "bully pulpit" marred his opening months and
reflected more troubling problems within the adminis-

tration. The man who had won the White House by focusing on a specific message in a disciplined way now seemed as though he was working hard but without a particular objective. An out-of-focus presidency came across clearly through the media for several months.

A serious mistake Clinton made early on was to think that he could go around the Washington journalistic community and speak to the American people in an unfiltered fashion, as he had so often during the campaign. The president's first formal news conference didn't take place until March 23, 1993—sixty-three days after he was sworn in and the longest period without a press conference for a newly elected, modern-day chief executive. Five days earlier at a dinner of the Radio & Television Correspondents, Clinton remarked, "You know why I can stiff you on the press conferences? Because Larry King liberated me by giving me to the American people directly." Lame joking aside, the statement signified an attitude that time and the real-world circumstances would change. Three months later, after several afternoon news conferences, the White House criticized ABC and CBS for *not* broadcasting Clinton's first prime-time meeting with Washington journalists. The lesson that new, unconventional methods of communication could not completely replace traditional techniques had been learned. But the knowledge had come at a price. There would need to be strategic balancing of conventional and unconventional activities to deliver a message to the public. Given the number of competing outlets of popular communication, occasions for news coverage needed to blend with talk-show formats or town meetings.

The hiring of David Gergen to be a White House counselor on May 29, 1993, was open acknowledgment of problems in presidential performance and portrayal. Adviser to three Republican presidents, including tenure as director of communications for Ronald Reagan,

Gergen left journalism to serve in a position connecting the critical realms of policy, politics, and communication. Until the Gergen appointment, there had been a lack of sensitivity to the way these areas intersected and influenced each other. Clinton himself, in response to a question May 14 about a decline in his approval rating, had said: ". . . I'm trying to do hard things, and I can't do hard things, and conduct an ongoing campaign at the same time." The fact of political life today is that a president to succeed must "do hard things" *and* "conduct an ongoing campaign" to accomplish anything of consequence. Salesmanship during speeches and through sessions with local or national media is an important element of statesmanship. Of course, one has to be promoting a proposal or plan of substance in which he believes. But changing a policy or program won't occur without some kind of focused, visible campaign. Transforming talk into action takes more talk—as well as an effort to gauge the consequences, substantive or symbolic, of these words and deeds. Clinton's natural gifts as a campaigner—if used appropriately—could ultimately become critical to his success.

In his first year as president, Clinton proved puzzling to the public because of the paradoxes he created in their minds. The methodical, sure-footed figure of the campaign appeared haphazard and stumbling in the White House, particularly with government appointments and the conduct of foreign affairs. The man-of-the-people image that seemed so genuine in 1992 gave way to what looked like an infatuation with glittery Hollywood types, and there was that infamous $200 haircut. The candidate who showed strength by keeping his distance from groups or organizations appeared as president to be influenced by outsiders and also willing to be pushed around by members of Congress. Most significantly perhaps, words that helped him win the election came back to haunt him when he said or did things to contradict them. What happened to the first hundred days of legislation to rival Franklin Roosevelt's, to the middle-class tax cut, to the emphasis on responsibilities, to the military assistance to stop the bloodshed in Bosnia, and the rest?

Confident and responsive regardless of the setting, Clinton's garrulousness and desire to enhance his political appeal contributed proportionately to public puzzlement. Reacting to one of the several modifications for dealing with homosexuals in the military, Democratic Representative Barney Frank of Massachusetts said of the president, "He thinks he can talk his way out of anything, and that's how he gets into trouble." Particularly with the easy access journalists now have to prior statements, what's been said before about a subject matters. Consistency might be the hobgoblin of little minds, as Emerson thought, but presidential leadership in this communications age means (among other things) the ability to convey a deliberate, continuing sense of command and control.

Paradoxical statements and actions suggest flux or indecision, disorienting the public. For instance, the word "change" might define Clinton's main theme or objective, but citizens need to understand precisely what "change" means and where this president—or any president— wants to take them. This is particularly important in the case of a politician who emerges quickly as a national figure, as now tends to happen with regularity. If the people don't really know a president in some depth— strengths, weaknesses, and everything else—they often wonder what to expect and become perplexed or disillusioned at policy shifts or contradictory utterances. In a much-publicized interview in *Rolling Stone* (December 9, 1993), Clinton repeatedly said he was "frustrated by the change-averse culture" of Washington, but he then lashed out with keep-the-kids-away fury that he'd "not gotten one damn bit of credit from the knee-jerk liberal press." One wonders if "the knee-jerk liberal press" doesn't want change, who does?

Moreover, in Clinton's case, conveying a sense of consistency is important because he lacks an easily identifiable ideology. At best he might be called an activist-pragmatist. Programs to create jobs or secure universal health care receive strong support from the liberally inclined, while a measure like the North American Free Trade Agreement (NAFTA) raised the blood pressure of many liberals and forced Clinton to rely on more conservative legislators for congressional action. Given such decisions, this activist-pragmatist has to work that much harder to produce shifting coalitions for his proposals. Allies and adversaries switch places, depending on the initiative.

Notwithstanding the successes after his early stumbling, Clinton's management style is open to criticism because of a lack of concentrated effort on a specific matter until a deadline looms. Instead of setting the agenda and pacing the work with controlled discipline, there's a frenzied rush at the end, prompting fast deals and compromises to win support. In late 1993, a senior White House official described the president as "a man who lies down in front of trains with great frequency and gets up at the last minute every time." Clinton's energy, intelligence, and forceful personality aside, it's difficult to imagine this trick working throughout his presidency.

With all of the ups and downs since Clinton's inauguration, instead of the ship of state it seems more accurate to think in terms of a roller-coaster. Accomplishments and question-raising setbacks (or revelations) take place within relatively brief periods of time, making it difficult for the public to form long-term judgments about him and his ability to govern. The fishiness of the "Whitewater affair" (a complicated real estate deal involving the Clintons while they lived in Arkansas) and White House floundering in responding to questions about what happened added to the president's early woes, shifting public attention away from the present or future to the murky past. With the scent of scandal in the air, it was not uncommon to hear journalists confuse the collective word "Whitewater" with another older, collective word, "Watergate."

To his credit, Clinton combined the rhetorical approach of Ronald Reagan and the insider arm-twisting of Lyndon Johnson to achieve the passage of NAFTA near the end of his first year in office. That triumph, engineered against great odds, as well as his work on gun control and other measures to combat crime and violence made the political community and the public at large see the president as a more commanding leader. He appeared now better able to use "the bully pulpit" to his advantage while also deftly pulling the individual levers of government in ways members of the House of Representatives and the Senate appreciate. However, with complicated and controversial initiatives about health care, welfare, and government restructuring facing the administration, sustaining the outside approach of Reagan *and* the inside method of Johnson will be critical to future success.

Effective White House leadership today requires judicious, even strategic, balancing of talk and action, of politicking and policy-making, of campaigning and governing, of principle and pragmatism, of domestic concerns and international affairs, of traditional practice and new initiatives, of pomp and just-folks occasions. It's not a matter of making either/or decisions about conducting the office. It's a continuing both/and situation. Finding the right proportion to emphasize at a certain time is critical. Over five centuries ago in *The Prince*, Machiavelli described the successful leader as someone able to combine the strength of a lion and the cunning of a fox. In today's vastly more complicated world, Machiavelli's perception still holds true, yet you also need deliberate and delicate juggling of several approaches and concerns to create purposeful and strong leadership. For Bill Clinton, winning the White House was grueling—but it was only the beginning of testings that would prove even more challenging.

I t was the best of times, it was the worst of times, it was the age of wisdom, it was the age of foolishness, it was the epoch of belief, it was the epoch of incredulity. . . .

Charles Dickens's famous comparison of contradictory superlatives could also serve as a suitable description of American political and media life in 1992. The accomplishments and blunders of political figures and people in popular communications created collective mood swings in the public. The "noisiest authorities" (Dickens's phrase) relied on received, conventional wisdom shaped by the recent past for many of their pronouncements, but the citizens were demanding and expecting something different.

That's one reason why the ins and out of Ross Perot had such an impact. His involvement was changing the way the media handled politics at the same time that he was changing presidential politics. The public saw Perot as a challenge to the established practices of the media and to the status quo politics of the two parties. As a result, Perot represented more than an independent, personality-centered candidacy, and reservations about him weren't as debilitating as they might have been. Even though almost 20 million people voted for him, many millions more saw genuine value in one individual's effort (albeit, in part, egotistical) to bring about institutional changes. To be sure, he was amusingly entertaining on most occasions—one newspaper's scorecard of the first presidential debate reported that the "live" audience in St. Louis laughed nine times, with Perot being responsible for eight of the responses, Clinton one, and Bush none. But Perot's broader message was more significant. A human lightning rod at a stormy time, he helped collect and subsequently divert much of the public anger, cynicism, and frustration. And his decision to make talk shows central to his campaign had a profound effect on the political process. Instead of a mediated monologue as we had seen in 1988 and earlier, with emphasis on short advertising spots and clipped candidate statements on the news, there was a more democratic dialogue in 1992, with people and their questions offering greater citizen connection to political life.

Perot, of course, doesn't deserve all the credit for changing the political media environment. Other figures and forces contributed. The efforts of Patrick Buchanan and Paul Tsongas in New Hampshire as well as Jerry Brown's low-money, high-volume six-month refrain of "taking back America" struck chords that resonated throughout the year. Particularly with what happened in New Hampshire, there were intimations that an angry and alienated electorate was anything but apathetic. Large crowds gathered to hear and quiz the candidates, and voting in the primary reached a remarkable 62 percent of those registered (or 42 percent of the voting-age population).

With character doubts nagging Clinton and Bush proving unbeatable (despite Buchanan's bloodying criticism), participation in subsequent primaries plummeted to an overall average (including New Hampshire) of about 20 percent of eligible voters. That number, however, is somewhat misleading because many of the state party contests took place as Perot's independent campaign took shape and received intense attention. Election officials across the country reported thousands of calls requesting information about how to go about voting for Perot in the primaries—which, of course, wasn't possible.

Perot's withdrawal in July produced another mood swing in the public, because as much as anything it signaled a return to traditional politics at a time when many were hoping and working for an alternative approach. Interest dove. During a round-table discussion involving scholars and journalists September 25, the distinguished historian Henry Graff lamented, "One of the things the press is not covering well is the general boredom of the public. Just who is reading all of this stuff the press writes? The press takes the temperature of these candidates daily and analyzes new segments of the two campaigns' presentation, which are often the same day after day. I find this very distressing. The public at large is not interested in the campaign."[16] Yet, six days later, Perot re-entered the race, and the word boredom wasn't used again to describe the public's feeling.

During the last month of the campaign, numbers reflect the intense citizen interest. Exact audience figures aren't knowable (C-SPAN, for example, is not counted by Nielsen Media Research), but the Commission on Presidential Debates estimated that there were 85 million watching the first debate, 89 million the second, and 97 million the third. The encounter of vice-presidential candidates drew 74 million. Perot's infomercials earned respectable ratings the twelve times they aired or were rebroadcast. His first such production (on CBS, October 6) finished second in competition with other network programs and was watched in 11.1 million homes. His CBS program on October 24 drew a smaller audience (9.1 million homes), but was the highest rated show in the time period. According to a special report of Nielsen Media Research, "Approximately 8.5 million households (13 million viewers) tuned in, during the average minute, to watch Perot's infomercials on ABC, CBS, and NBC."[17]

Some 76 percent of the respondents to a *New York Times*/CBS News Poll in October said the presidential race was interesting—a figure that compared to 40 percent in 1988 and 56 percent in 1984. Across America, people were following what the candidates said and did with a concern bordering on fascination. The television audience for the third presidential debate was particularly intriguing—and, indeed, satisfying for anyone who longs for democracy with an informed citizenry. That debate (on a Monday) began at seven p.m. in the East, six in the Midwest, and four on the West Coast. Just imagine what viewership would have been later in the evening. Besides the attraction of political programs on television screens, Perot's book, *United We Stand*, and Al Gore's environmental study, *Earth in the Balance*, both occupied places on the best-seller lists.

Although apathy from voter alienation or boredom had been the predicted fear a few months earlier, the intense interest in the campaign and candidates at the end resulted in the highest electoral turnout (in terms of percentage of voting age population actually voting) since the convulsive, war-focused 1968 race involving Richard Nixon, Hubert Humphrey, and George Wallace. The Federal Election Commission reported that 55.24 percent of the voting age population went to the polls—over 5 percent more than had voted in 1988 and a little more than 5 percent fewer than 1968. A total of 104,426,659 people voted in 1992—compared to 91,594,693 in 1988 and 73,211,875 in 1968.

In a post-election study conducted by the Times Mirror Center for The People & The Press, 77 percent of Americans said they learned enough to make an informed voting choice, a rise of 18 percent over 1988. Seventy percent of the respondents said the debates were particularly helpful in deciding for whom to vote, that percentage in contrast to 48 percent in 1988. In grading their own civic conduct, 61 percent gave "voters" a grade of "A" or "B" in the survey—as compared to 49 percent four years before. Even the public's opinion of media coverage improved, 36 percent awarding "A's" or "B's" (a 6 percent rise from 1988) and an increase amid much controversy over whether there was press bias against Bush in 1992.

In exit polling reported on CBS during its election night coverage, the ranking of sources influencing presidential voting in 1992 was 1) debates, 2) talk shows, 3) convention coverage, and 4) commercials, with the debates beating ads almost three to one. The longer forms of political communication won out over the highly compressed variety, with citizens themselves feeling better about how they became informed and the campaign in general. The mud of 1988 had been washed away by civic interest and involvement. Negative commercials and attack ads appeared throughout the fall—one study documented that of Clinton's twenty-four spots eleven were negative and of Bush's fifteen a total of twelve were negative, with nine of them raising questions about his opponent's character—but they had minimal impact and did not drive down voting. The standard thinking about the consequences of such appeals ended up like the year's other conventional wisdom—on its head and of little help in understanding the specific impact of this aspect of political communication on the public.

In 1992, it almost seemed as though all the attention to negative advertising in the aftermath of the previous election resulted in the public becoming desensitized to these messages. They were a regular part of the larger

political media environment, yet a secondary consideration. And the news media, with their "ad-watch"
features, exposed some of the shenanigans and questionable material related to many of the commercials.
Interestingly, four years earlier, according to a study of
the Markle Commission on the Media and the Electorate, "the Bush campaign was the single most important
source of influence on voters, largely through the use of
advertising. Very little paid political advertising by either
camp [Bush or Dukakis], however, dealt with issues that
concerned voters such as the budget deficit, drugs or
health care."[18]

The rising and falling levels of citizen interest during
1992 made the race unlike any other in recent memory.
The absorption of the public in the last month put the
lie to the notion that (because of new campaign and
communication techniques) voters are now overly ma-
nipulated or overwhelmed by all the information to
the point of not thinking about it. As Samuel L. Popkin
argues in *The Reasoning Voter*, a book which appeared
just before the campaign, citizens might not possess a
vast amount of detailed political or governmental knowledge, but they are forever processing information about
politics that leads to reasoned opinions and judgments.
A rigorous, refreshing rebuttal of what's usually said
about the citizenry's political awareness, *The Reasoning
Voter* proves that Americans take more than echoes of
slogans and sound-bites or haunting video images into
voting booths. Popkin, a political scientist with experience as a campaign consultant and polling analyst for
CBS News, writes:

> Voting is not a reflexive, mechanistic use of daily-life
> or media information. It involves reasoning, the con-
> necting of some information to government perform-
> ance and other information to specific government

policies. People do not reason directly from personal problems to votes; they reason with ideas about governmental performance and responsibility. They consider not only economic issues but family, residential, and consumer issues as well. They think not only of their immediate needs but also of their needs for insurance against future problems; not only about private goods but also about collective goods. They think not only of how they are doing but also about how other people like themselves are doing; not just about the immediate future but also about the long term.[19]

Popkin acknowledges that the public is inclined to take "cues" and "information shortcuts" in dealing with political messages of various kinds. This "low-information rationality," however, combines with someone's real-world experience to form a person's political frame of mind. How the man or woman reacts at the polls is a complicated, individualistic matter, especially with today's emphasis on personality- or candidate-centered politics and the greater inclination to electoral independence as well as ticket-splitting.

Compounding the complexity of the voter's civic work is the fact (not stressed as much as it should be) that each election has its own defining characteristics and circumstances. In broadbrush historical terms, the presidential campaigns of 1960, 1968, and 1980 were driven by large, substantive issues about the country's direction or choices that needed democratic resolution. Other elections since 1960 were in their way significant, but they seemed to possess less weight of content. For example, the campaigns of 1984 and 1988 were to a considerable degree referendums on whether to continue what Ronald Reagan's victory in 1980 had set in motion. It became clear before 1992's political activity began in earnest that the public understood the high stakes involved in choosing a president. The anger, frustration, and discontent were signs of a big election in the making, and the subsequent attentiveness to the different kinds of political messages confirmed how important citizens perceived this presidential decision to be.

Considerations about the economy, job potentials, and health care helped frame the discourse, but never far from the campaign's speeches or discussions was growing public concern about the government's deficit and mounting debt. "We live by symbols," Justice Oliver Wendell Holmes once remarked. The deficit and debt had become twin and entwined symbols in the minds of many people signifying government profligacy and mismanagement. With their "low-information rationality," citizens might not have an economist's understanding of the different factors contributing to the deficit and debt or to the ultimate consequences of these conditions. All the red ink, though, was a red flag of warning—the country's economic future stood in jeopardy if government spending continued to race beyond government revenues. Some people even saw the yearly deficits leading to the $4 trillion debt as the enemy replacing Communism as a threat to America.

The public mind thus concentrated, it is a short step to view the federal government with a jaundiced eye and to want definite action to slay or at least cripple the enemy. What's at risk if nothing dramatically different happens is another symbol: the American dream, the powerful national idea (and ideal) of people achieving prosperity that leads to even greater success for future generations. In 1992, Paul Tsongas was the first serious political messenger to make an argument for the need to act. After he dropped out, Ross Perot made it a centerpiece of his campaign—amplifying as well as clarifying the situation with both direct talk and his ever-handy series of charts.

Thanks to Perot's efforts, the other candidates were forced to address the problems, and the public learned much more than the Republicans or Democrats probably wanted them to know. That Martin L. Gross's *The Government Racket: Washington Waste from A to Z* became a best-selling book is another illustration of how seriously people were taking the subject.

It's, of course, too early to tell whether the high-stakes campaign of 1992 will be regarded as a watershed election with long-term effects that contribute to a reshaping of American political thinking and action. In *Boiling Point*, Kevin Phillips makes the case that in order for 1992 to join the select company of previous watershed races (1800, 1828, 1896, 1932, and 1968) Bill Clinton and his administration will have to achieve "nothing less than the economic renewal of the United States and its worried middle class."[20] A vital, vigorous center is crucial to America's future for the remainder of this century and beyond. Clinton's one-note call for "change" during the campaign faced the almost daily test of execution following his inauguration. In the wake of the Senate's defeat of his proposed economic stimulus package in the spring of 1993, the president confessed, "I must say there's a lot I have to learn about this town"—meaning, of course, Washington and its competing realms of influence and power. In other words, political talk about "change" is one thing; political action of which identifiable political watersheds are made is another, and much harder to accomplish.

History will render its verdict about the Clinton presidency in due course. Clearly, though, the year that led to Clinton's occupancy of the White House marked a watershed in political campaigning. In demanding different and extended sources of information, citizens helped bring about a more direct, democratized kind of communication that responded to their questions and concerns in a sustained, continuing way. Journalists played their part and they remained significant, but many barriers came down to allow the public at large greater, two-way involvement.

American political life was continuing to evolve from what it once had been. During the party-strong nineteenth century, there had been a profound reluctance of having presidential candidates personally involved in the process of seeking votes. The parties themselves took responsibility for national campaigns, and partisan newspapers circulated candidates' views. But beginning early in the twentieth century, there was a shift from the approach of stand-back-from-the-people republicanism to a more open, democratic practice. By this time parties were no longer as important as they had been. Individual political personalities, especially Theodore Roosevelt, captured people's attention, stimulating interest in politicians' public and private lives. Primaries were invented, making selection of candidates subject to democratic choice. And advertising, the bolder the better, became a preferred way to deliver political messages.

In his authoritative study *See How They Ran*, Gil Troy, a historian, traces the movement from republican restraint to democratic devotion. As he works his way through this century, it's almost as though each succeeding campaign compelled candidates to do more traveling, speaking, and handshaking. Vestiges of republicanism remained, notably a concern for character and virtue, but the phrase "running for president" became more literal than metaphorical. Describing high-minded Adlai Stevenson's private distaste for new electoral techniques in 1956, Troy writes:

> Never before had presidential candidates sought out the voters so aggressively. Although campaigning rituals had the nominee appear as a mendicant in

search of a voter's favor, the people always approached the candidate at rallies, train stations, prop-stops, and motorcades. Now the candidate was a beggar, stalking voters between lingerie counters in department stores. Privately, Stevenson agonized. "No one worthy of being President should act like a panhandler," he snapped. One day, after wriggling into a cowboy outfit to lead a parade, Stevenson sighed: "*God*, what a man won't do to get public office."[21]

The democratic distance has been reduced considerably during the last four decades. But what happened in 1992 demonstrated that the sideshow silliness of dressing up like a cowboy can be—and should be—replaced by thorough, probing discussions of issues affecting the lives and destinies of the people. New communication formats made possible by sophisticated modern technology now link candidates to citizens in a democratic dialogue that no doubt will be enhanced and enlarged in the years to come. Charles Dickens's flowing sentence to begin *A Tale of Two Cities* offers an apt description of 1992, but the haunting two words on the title page of E. M. Forster's novel *Howards End* provide the real lesson of 1992 and of the future: "Only connect. . ."

Part Two

Looking Forward

Fool's errand though it might be, attempting to describe the political media landscape looming on the horizon needs to take into account the forces of change that gathered speed and power in 1992—and continued to swirl after that year's Election Day. Until 1992, television dominated American political life by imposing certain medium-enhancing conventions on those seeking high elective office. Be entertaining, be pithy, be visually arresting, the consultants urged after learning what helped to ensure news coverage and effective advertising.

However, during the pivotal year of 1992, the body politic seemed to rebel against both the established conventions and the 1980s perception of the public as a lumpy mass of passive couch potatoes. From the primary campaigning in New Hampshire through the fall, the people seemed to be groping for whatever might be different from and better than before—new ideas, new modes of expression, new political players, even new possibilities beyond the traditional two candidates in the general election. For the first time since 1912 (and Theodore Roosevelt was a special case that year), an alternative to the clout of the Democratic and Republican parties boldly emerged by capitalizing on this rebellious mood. Major party solidity, which governed American politics for so much of the century, was being challenged at the same time the dominant means of political communication was facing public questioning and impending institutional upheaval.

With citizens clearly wanting greater connection to their political life, it's anything but idle musing to wonder what role ever more sophisticated communications technology will play in American democracy as a new century approaches. Were the strikingly different occurrences in 1992 the prelude to changes so profound that traditional ways of thinking and acting politically will become obsolete? Are we embarking on a new course of what it means to be a citizen of the United States?

Bill Clinton's victorious presidential campaign, coupled with Ross Perot's vote-getting performance, reflected not only a strong desire for change but also a rejection of the existing political leadership represented by George Bush. When viewed with detachment from the personalities involved, the dual motivation signifies an uneasy, unsettled electorate. Doubts that have been forming during recent years just don't seem to go away and, in fact, they fester, resulting in fear or worry about the future. Three decades ago, when survey researchers at the University of Michigan asked whether Washington could be trusted to do what's right most of the time, 62 percent of the people polled responded favorably. That was 1964. In 1992, the percentage had dropped to 26. Six months into 1993 and the Clinton Administration, *The Los Angeles Times* conducted a similar study and the number fell to only 14 percent, with 54 percent answering "some of the time" and 31 percent saying "hardly ever." A *Wall Street Journal*/NBC News poll released at the end of 1993 reported the same number of 14 percent believing that Washington would do the right thing all or most of the time. The newspaper provided the figure in a series, "Beltway Bog," which described what was called "the cynicism industry" in depressingly engrossing detail. This growing lack of trust symbolizes an absence of political faith and has ominous implications for the future. How can popular self-government effectively do its work in a climate of profound distrust and what's seemingly become chronic national cynicism. At what point do citizens collectively say, "Enough is enough"?

A critical first step in restoring trust and making Americans more confident politically involves the bringing together of the two worlds of campaigning and governing. Back in January 1990, when David S. Broder of *The Washington Post* began his personal effort to reduce disillusionment and cynicism, he wrote: "We have to help reconnect politics and government—what happens in the campaign and what happens afterward in public policy— if we are to have accountability by our elected officials and genuine democracy in this country." In this column and subsequent ones, Broder sought to improve American political life for the mid-term election of 1990 and beyond. He, however, was in part motivated by what had happened in 1988, especially the presidential race between George Bush and Michael Dukakis.

The week Bush took up residence in the White House in 1989, he was asked by Barbara Walters of ABC News about his winning-yet-controversial campaign. "That's history," Bush remarked. "That doesn't mean anything anymore." Such a cavalier dismissal can be interpreted a number of ways, but during the next four years that campaign did prove to mean a great deal. Take, for example, the Bush pledge and surefire applause line as he stumped the country in 1988: "Read my lips: No new taxes." The first utterance of these six words took place in

Bush's acceptance speech at the Republican National Convention when he said: ". . . my opponent [Michael Dukakis] won't rule out raising taxes. But I will and the Congress will push me to raise taxes, and I'll say no, and they'll push, and I'll say no, and they'll push again. And I'll say to them, Read my lips: No new taxes."

The slogan started to haunt Bush and his presidency in 1990, when he, indeed, agreed to tax increases worked out by members of Congress and his administration. "Dirty Harry" of the Clint Eastwood movies might never back down, but real political life was different. In a series of articles for *The Washington Post* a month before the 1992 election, Bob Woodward traced how the slogan came into being and why its pledge had to be broken. According to Woodward's reporting, politically motivated campaign consultants battled with policy-oriented advisers over whether to include the line, drafted by speechwriter Peggy Noonan. After much internal debate, the political players (led by advertising and media heavyweight Roger Ailes) prevailed. The principal argument for keeping it had little to do with future governance, particularly in the critical areas of taxing and spending. There were more important campaign concerns. "The wimp image had to be buried," Woodward wrote, and a lip-curled, no-nonsense movie line had sound-bite potential. The slogan did help Bush in the campaign, but abandoning the pledge two years later seriously hurt him for his race in 1992. That's history, as the former president might say.

Emphasizing that citizens wouldn't have to worry about new federal taxes was just one of the decisions by Bush and his staff for a political advantage in 1988. There were others. In *At the Highest Levels: The Inside Story of the End of the Cold War*, Michael R. Beschloss and Strobe Talbott recount Bush's campaign strategy for dealing with the Soviet Union. Talking with Mikhail Gorbachev during the Soviet leader's first visit to America in

December 1987, Vice President Bush warned Gorbachev about tough, partisan talk during the upcoming presidential contest. Beschloss and Talbott write:

> Even though the presidential election year of 1988 would not begin for another three weeks, the vice president was already campaigning hard for the Republican nomination. His party's Senate leader, Robert Dole of Kansas, was running ahead of him in several polls.
>
> Bush said, "There's a good chance that I'm going to win the presidential election next year. Dole looks pretty dangerous right now, but I think I'll get the Republican nomination. If I'm elected—and I think I will be—you should understand that I want to improve our relations."
>
> Bush said that during his seven years as Ronald Reagan's vice president, he had had to keep his moderate views to himself. He explained that Reagan was surrounded by "marginal intellectual thugs" who would be delighted to seize on any evidence that the vice president was a closet liberal. Therefore, during the 1988 campaign, he would have to do and say many things to get elected. Mr. Gorbachev should ignore them.
>
> Gorbachev said that he understood. Long afterward, he recalled this conversation as the "most important talk Bush and I ever had." Over the next four years, each time the Soviet leader's close aides complained that Bush was pandering to Republican conservatives, Gorbachev would remind them of their talk in the limousine, saying, "Don't worry. His heart is in the right place."[1]

Breaking pledges and engaging in image-enhancing pandering aren't exactly new phenomena in American political life. However, people in politics and journalism as well as the public at large need to do much more to establish stronger connections between modern-day campaigning and day-to-day governing. At times nowadays, the activities seem to have too little relationship to each other. Short-term political objectives often take precedence over longer-range policy proposals for more effective governance. If journalists in their reporting could present what they are able to learn about the merits and consequences of campaign statements to actual governing, then citizens would better understand the necessary connections and be more able to form reasoned judgments.

To a degree, of course, such an approach involves continual probing for links the public might miss in the theatrical hoopla of a campaign. The explicit connections require emphasis and repetition. Bush ultimately paid a price for his 1988 campaign, and Clinton learned quickly as president that campaign statements (about, for example, a middle-class tax cut, balancing the budget, and breaking gridlock for rapid governmental action) are not forgotten as soon as the ballots are counted. Clinton adviser George Stephanopoulos lamented in the summer of 1993, "We have become hostage to Lexis-Nexis," but it's more than having easy access to a candidate's words in a computer retrieval system—or what Stephanopoulos called "an excess of literalism." It's really a matter of taking campaigns seriously and conducting them with a stronger commitment to actually serving in office.

Campaigns should be a political prelude to governmental performance—and not a limited-run extravaganza concluding on Election Day. Current conventional wisdom says that governing now involves engaging in a permanent campaign that builds public support in ways similar to real political campaigns—polling, focus groups, scripted media events, and so on. But, for the sake of improving citizen trust, campaigns themselves should take place in closer proximity to the prospect of governing. Reducing the distance that now exists has to be a primary objective in the future. Focused, substantive coverage of candidates and what happens during campaigns can close the gap and enable citizens to form their opinions with the most relevant information. This kind of journalism is more difficult than reporting the day's events from the campaign trail. It necessitates connecting what a candidate says to governmental policy and practice. If a proposal seems overly fanciful or appealing in the abstract but in reality is removed from the realm of possibility, analysis reflecting doubt deserves strong play or airing. Such work offers a dual warning to a candidate that a campaign needs to be closely tied to governing and to a citizen that a candidate might be promising or even pandering with the election's outcome the principal concern.

One reason campaigning and governing seem to spin in separate orbits is the current electoral system. With the decline of party insiders having a say in selecting candidates, the nominating process is simultaneously more open to public participation and to efforts of deception by political aspirants. A virtue of stuffy, smoke-filled rooms of bygone days was candid discussion of a person's strengths and weaknesses by people who knew the person well and could speculate on future governmental performance. Today an individual looks in a mirror and sees a future president, governor, senator, whatever, and it's a decision of self-selection that leads to candidate-centered races. The party's in the background, with the focus on the individual competing for the nomination and, if successful in winning that, for the office being sought in the general election.

Though clearly more democratic in terms of participation by the populace, such a system puts greater responsibility on citizens to judge the merits of political figures. This means that what happens during campaigns take on more meaning. Evaluation to a considerable degree comes from exposure to and assessment of the different kinds of communication a candidate uses. For the future to be different from the past—and for the public to be better served—there needs to be more deliberate attention given to political communication. In this circumstance prediction and prescription converge. As media-delivered ads, speeches, town-meeting discussions, and debates occupy the central place in the campaign process, it's time that those responsible for devising and overseeing the electoral system recognize this fact and act to enhance democracy.

Somewhere between a half to three-quarters of the budget for a major-office campaign today goes into preparing and airing commercials on television and radio. At the same time when media messages have increasingly become principal vehicles of political communication, campaign costs have skyrocketed, with broadcast stations and networks conspicuous beneficiaries. On the Congressional level, winning a seat in the House of Representatives in 1976 required spending an average of $87,200, while election to the Senate cost $609,100. In 1992, the averages for winners jumped to $549,963 in the House and $3,552,040 in the Senate. More expenses, of course, mean more attention to fund-raising. According to the Federal Election Commission, New York Senator Al D'Amato helped finance his 1992 re-election—which cost $9,175,533—by collecting an average of $62,819 per week during the last two years of his term. Senator Phil Gramm of Texas averaged $111,792 each week in contributions for the two years before he was re-elected in 1990.

Some other dollar amounts suggest that money may not be the mother's milk of politics, as the cliché goes, so much as the most expensive champagne, complete with certain side-effects if consumed in quantity. Accounting by the Federal Election Commission after campaign activities in 1992 showed that California Democrats Barbara Boxer and Dianne Feinstein spent, respectively, $10,368,600 and $8,054,222 to win their Senate seats that year. Their opponents, Bruce Herschensohn and John Seymour, had campaign expenses of $7,649,072 and $6,849,805. That's $25,672,699 for the four candidates, and doesn't even count the money spent by their primary challengers. Democrat Mel Levine ran up charges of $7,195,444, Republican Thomas J. Campbell $5,106,273, Republican William E. Dannemeyer $3,531,716, Democrat Leo T. McCarthy $3,039,891, and Democrat Gray Davis $2,559,298. In 1992, thirty-four seekers of Senate seats spent over $3 million, while some fifty House candidates shelled out over $1 million trying to get elected. (On March 2, 1994, *The Wall Street Journal* reported that Senator Feinstein needed to raise $22,000 a day for her 1994 re-election bid.)

There's an unseemly quality to the quantities of money raised and spent. Despite protestations from politicians to the contrary, citizens believe that sizable gifts buy access for the provider—a meeting to discuss pending legislation, personal attention to a written request, or worse. All of the dollars that flow in and out of political life nowadays contribute to the public's distrust and disillusionment. The moneyed involvement in politics of savings and loan wheeler-dealer Charles Keating is a vivid recent example of one person's actions and their impact on what people think. For the sake of the future and a return to more civic faith in American democracy, how political money is received and spent deserves both reconsideration and reform. Suggested remedies abound: public financing of campaigns, voluntary spending limits, relatively cheap—or even free—television time, to name just a few.

With a widespread attitude that something must be
done, one might imagine that changing a criticized and
controversial system would be a principal priority for
elected officials. In recent years, however, much of the
talk of significant reform has taken place during or shortly
after campaigns, with little or nothing actually happening
at other times to improve the situation. That public financing of presidential contests came into being as a
consequence of the misdeeds surrounding Richard
Nixon's re-election effort of 1972 shows how a profound
occurrence can prompt meaningful action. But enduring
another Watergate-level experience seems a high price to
pay for campaign reform, especially for those seeking
places in the Senate or House of Representatives.
Whether public anger and dissatisfaction about politics-
as-usual will lead to anything beyond some superficial
changes is a genuine concern. Unfortunately, the combi-
nation of incumbent self-interest and politically motivated special interests seem to conspire against the
public's interest in removing big money (and what that
connotes) from political life.

Be that as it may, it's worth remembering that three incumbent presidents (Gerald Ford, Jimmy Carter, and
George Bush) have lost to challengers since public financing came into being for the nation's highest office in
1976. (Ronald Reagan is the only victorious incumbent
in this period, while the 1988 race didn't involve a sitting
president.) Establishing a system that includes acceptance of public funds and strict compliance with voluntary
spending limits is a logical starting point to end what's
aptly called "the money chase" in politics. Such provi-
sions could be worked out at the local or state levels, too,
but there's a genuinely more compelling need to do
something for House and Senate contests.

In 1992, according to the Federal Election Commission, incumbent senators received an average of

$4,520,394 in contributions in contrast to their challeng-
ers with $1,861,181, while House incumbents had cam-
paign expense money of $582,330 compared to $154,607
for their opponents. Clearly, greater equity in funding
would make races more competitive. Raising the possibility of public financing is risky, of course, given the
mood of so many people about higher taxes and the
generally low regard for Congress. (A *Wall Street Journal*/NBC News poll in late 1993 showed that 65 percent
of those surveyed disapproved of the job Congress was
doing, while only 24 percent approved.) And just imagine how certain radio and television talk-show hosts
would react to any serious possibility of public funding.

However, it's critical for the future and civic well-
being to resolve several questions about who should pay
the costs required to participate in the nation's political
life. Should people of means have a decided advantage
by bankrolling their own involvement or that of people
they want in office? Do we want the special interests
with their political action committees to continue to finance candidates they might be able to influence as
office-holders? (In 1992, House incumbents received an
average of $261,976 from PACs, while challengers got
an average of $27,621 in PAC money—almost a ten to
one difference.) Is it politically fair or democratically
healthy to have conspicuous imbalance in campaigns?
There would be fewer calls for term limits if the election
system was less favorable to incumbents and more ac-
commodating to challengers. Some form of public
financing that's linked to voluntary spending limits would
help purify how money flows to candidates and control
what dollars are available to spend.

Given the significance of broadcast communication in
modern political life, serious campaign reform should
also deal straightforwardly with advertising and other
forums for delivering messages of candidates to the

public. For example, advertising charges for television and radio commercials could be reduced to the lowest possible rate for anyone complying with the spending limit. It's possible, too, to treat ads that feature direct, personal appeals from the candidate differently. Why not let the candidate speak for a full minute but charge the cost of a thirty-second spot? This measure would allow for fuller statements of a politician's proposals and qualifications. There's a chance, too, that such an arrangement might help reduce the number of negative or attack ads that run with minimal acknowledgment of who's responsible for the message. In addition, if an individual or group operating outside of a campaign decides to sponsor commercials, the candidate being supported should be accountable for these messages. Requiring a signed statement from the candidate involved is one way to link the outsider's advertising to the campaign.

Making free air-time available is another possibility for curbing costs and for providing political information to the citizenry. Some proposals advocate the awarding of a certain number of hours to the two major political parties, with party officials deciding which candidates will appear and why. Such a plan could work to assist politicians on the national, state, or local levels. In the realm of presidential politics, you find a number of definite ideas. In *See How They Run: Electing the President in an Age of Mediaocracy* and in an essay, "Political Coverage in the 1990s: Teaching the Old News New Tricks," Paul Taylor sketches out what he calls "a five-minute fix." He writes: "Each candidate for president should be given five minutes of free time a night, on alternating nights, simultaneously on every television and radio station in the country for the final five weeks of the presidential campaign."[2]

Some kind of arrangement that blends party involvement (to cover other elective offices) and presidential candidates would help enlighten potential voters, but it's difficult to imagine agreement from the broadcasting industry over free time, and independent or third-party candidates might bedevil the working out of details. Candidate-centered campaigns, similar to Ross Perot's effort in 1992, could become much more commonplace in political races up and down the ticket, especially if the major parties continue to languish as institutions.

Regardless of the precise rules governing political advertising in the future, monitoring of these messages by journalists serves a useful function and should be expanded to be a more prominent feature of coverage. As the often-repeated line goes, a modern political rally involves three or four people sitting in front of a television. Analyzing how candidates and campaigns present themselves—and their opponents—offers the public context for evaluation. Are the statements true? Is relevant information avoided? How possible is the promise? In addition, new communication technologies are able to transform images without the average person being aware, meaning non-partisan analysts or critics need to be watching political spots even more closely. What's called "morphing" allows one image to be changed into another by a computer. This digital manipulation of images can (among other things) alter the color of hair or eyes, the size of a person, or someone's facial expression. The computer-generated image cannot be distinguished from a real image. Such technology could become a playground for unprincipled political advertisers—which means that all of their work deserves closer scrutiny and sharp criticism when warranted.

How candidates advertise themselves and their views is just one domain of political communication in need of continuing attention as well as purposeful reform. Campaign debates are also well worth more discussion and possible formal action. Again in 1992, as seems to happen with quadrennial regularity, wrangling over presidential and vice-presidential debates became a noisy distraction at the time when millions of citizens were starting to focus seriously on the race. Jousting over the number, timing, format, and other details of the debates eventually resulted in four meetings with varying ground rules over nine days between October 11 and 19. Despite the one-on-top-of-the-other quality of these debates—some commentators likened the situation to a political mini-series—the occasions attracted huge audiences and generated public interest that seemed both genuine and admirable. What was said or done during the debates was a principal subject of conversation across America, and their value of offering extended looks at the candidates in relation to each other was without question.

In most cases, as happened in 1992, direct comparisons from debates can help frame a campaign, with television providing the collective vantage point. Of course, it's important to recognize the different dimensions of debates. They are political, informational, theatrical, and—yes—gladiatorial occasions. But substance and style intertwine themselves in revealing ways. Cogent, clear, concise statements delivered in a sincere, spontaneous manner are worth more than debating points. Such statements can suggest both leadership qualities and a sense of self that citizens find reassuring.

Looked at realistically, political debating on television is very much a balancing act. It's a test under pressure of a candidate's ability to control a situation while projecting definite personal qualities. On an individual level, the balancing takes place as the candidate attempts to appear intelligent without being intellectual, confident without being cocky, assertive without being autocratic, determined without being defensive. In addition, whatever's said needs to reflect fluency about an issue, but avoid a fog of facts obscuring larger beliefs or principles. Debates can help answer the critical question: What convictions drive a candidate? Body language, too, plays a role in a citizen's assessment. Such factors as poise, facial expressions, eye contact, and hand movement contribute to an overall perception of executive stature—or lack thereof. Shifty eyes or a shaky voice speak for themselves.

On the presidential level, debates offer the nation lengthy exposure to those seeking to lead the country. With their regularity since 1976, they've become something of a political and media yardstick for measuring major candidates. The words spoken and the physical gestures converge to help form what Walter Lippmann called "the pictures in our heads."

Do we make too much of the debates as tests for those seeking to govern America? Are rhetorical and dramatic skills unduly emphasized? Harry Truman once said: "I sit here all day trying to persuade people to do the things they ought to have sense enough to do without my persuading them. . . . That's all the powers of the President amount to." In this case, Truman understated reality. However, in the contemporary political and media environment that blends statecraft with stagecraft, the power to persuade via the television airwaves is an important dimension of effective political leadership. We get some hints or indications of a public figure's ability in this area from a series of serious debates.

Given the standing in the public mind of these particular political occasions, there is an ongoing debate over the debates, especially whether legislation should be adopted formally mandating a series of debates. Representative Edward J. Markey of Massachusetts has introduced bills in Congress linking the acceptance of federal campaign funds to participation in debates. As he told a conference on "The Future of Presidential Debates" in February 1993, "Last year voters shelled out $110 million in general-election funds. It seems to me that five debates [four presidential and one vice-presidential] is the least the candidates can do in return. The voters want these debates, and the reluctance of the major parties to embrace them is one of the reasons that too many voters have lost faith in the political process."[3]

An opposing viewpoint is held by Newton N. Minow, the director of the Annenberg Washington Program in Communications Policy Studies of Northwestern University, who said in testimony before a House subcommittee, "Because the debates [in 1992] proved so valuable to the electorate, the haphazard nature of their planning is worrisome. I question, though, whether legislation is the answer. Our political campaigns are already over-littered with regulations; we should impose new ones only when the problem is dire, and its solution, unequivocal. Caution seems advisable in light of the Law of Unintended Consequences, which so often mocks our efforts at political reform. I also question whether such a statute could realistically be enforced, and whether it could be harmonized with the First Amendment."[4] Minow, a former chairman of the Federal Communications Commission and respected commentator on political communication, raises legitimate concerns. However, attaching some formal strings to the public's campaign money doesn't seem too much to ask. In fact, it's relatively simple: No debates, no dough.

Legal precedent for such action already exists. Gubernatorial candidates in New Jersey who accept public funds for campaigning are required to debate twice before the general election. It's possible, too, to make this provision an aspect of any campaign financing legislation on the national, state, or local level.

As we've seen so often in recent years, when arranged effectively and fairly conducted, debates afford an opportunity to look at each candidate in a sustained way. Prospective voters receive more than a slogan, a ten-second sound-bite, or a thirty-second pitch. Some critics might argue that candidates merely deliver rehearsed lines when offering statements or responding to questions. Such criticism, though, doesn't recognize the decline of commonly shared political information that has occurred since 1980. With so many communication outlets competing for our time, it's no longer possible to take for granted that most of the citizenry know a candidate's views. Having a series of methodically planned debates, carried by a large number of different outlets simultaneously, would bring people together at specific times to hear what the candidates think and where they stand. Meaningful debates could well be the greatest recompense citizens receive for their public funding. In the years ahead, should no mandate come into effect, continued jockeying over debates might make campaigns more of a horse race—but voters could ultimately end up being the losers.

Looking to the future, it is probably either unrealistic or unduly optimistic to expect enactment of the structural reforms the presidential selection process so desperately needs. Primaries and caucuses that expand democracy and bring citizens into more direct, consistent relationship with their political life have merit. However, the haphazard arrangement of the primaries and caucuses leading to a presidential nomination continues to raise serious questions about a system that looks like it might have been designed by the cartoonist Rube Goldberg in his most inspired state of convolution. Its intimidating complexity makes public understanding difficult. Its state-dictated chronology (with such states as Iowa, New Hampshire, Maine, South Dakota, and Alaska the first places of competition) is unrepresentative demographically and democratically unfair to citizens in other larger states with urban areas. In addition, the news media tend to nationalize the early encounters, when the concerns and voting decisions might be more parochial in nature.

What happened in 1992 reflects the vagaries of the current system. The Iowa caucus, which had been newsworthy and consequential in most races since 1976, had no national relevance and generated little coverage because Iowa Democratic Senator Tom Harkin was in the race. With Harkin's statewide organization eager to engineer a landslide, media (and public) interest shifted to New Hampshire. There, a neighbor from Massachusetts (Paul Tsongas) had an advantage over the other Democratic candidates, including Bill Clinton, who at the time was trying to weather charges of adultery and avoiding the draft. There, too, economic conditions were worse than elsewhere in the country—meaning that George Bush, as incumbent president, had to campaign in a considerably more hostile environment and against a gifted emotion-rouser, Pat Buchanan. As it turned out, Clinton thought he did well enough in finishing second to call himself "the Comeback Kid," while Buchanan received an enormous amount of coverage—and with it came the implication of Bush's vulnerability—when early exit polling indicated the pundit-turned-politician would win 47 percent of the vote. When all the votes were counted Buchanan actually won 37 percent, but that fact seemed to get lost amid the chatter about what to expect in the upcoming state skirmishes.

The variability of the selection system was enhanced in the fall of 1993. Ohio Governor George Voinovich signed into law legislation that shifts his state's presidential primary from May to the same Tuesday in March when Illinois and Michigan conduct their primaries, creating something akin to a Midwestern primary day. In addition, California Governor Pete Wilson signed into law a bill that sets the 1996 primary in his state for the fourth Tuesday in March rather than the traditional first Tuesday in June. Having the California primary so much earlier will have a considerable impact on campaign strategy and possibly even affect the decisions of potential candidates. Given the state's size, a politician who's good on television and can afford several million dollars to broadcast commercials will be at a distinct advantage. Worried about being upstaged, Governor Mario Cuomo in his 1994 State of the State speech proposed moving New York's 1996 primary to March 5, the earliest date possible under Democratic Party rules and a month earlier than usual. Cuomo's suggestion sent California political figures to thinking about further change before the next presidential campaign.

Whatever finally happens with the primary in the nation's most populous state in 1996, there's a chance other states will want to schedule their primaries and caucuses on dates that are more advantageous to them in the years to come. The patchwork, every-state-for-itself quality to the arrangement somehow doesn't seem very helpful to selecting the best nominees for the highest national office. That's why a series of regional primaries or some kind of national primary (possibly following a national caucus or convention) make greater sense and need more serious deliberation in the future.[5] The candidates we get are the products of a specific process. If the process has flaws, chances are the flaws will be reflected in the products (or candidates) that emerge.

Shortly after the 1964 campaign, the news division of NBC assembled "a candid portrait" of the presidential race in words and pictures. Featuring a prologue by David Brinkley and an epilogue by Chet Huntley, the title of the book was *Somehow It Works*. A cartoon sketch of a befuddled, bedraggled citizen appears on the cover.[6] The phrase "somehow it works" still applies in describing the American political process on the presidential level, but increasingly one wonders how long the public will think so. Back in 1964, there was more trust in government and what politicians did—and the system had not been "reformed" to include all of the primaries and caucuses. Figuring out a more logical, representative, and comprehensible way of selecting presidents would be a large step in the direction of achieving more faith in the nation's government and its democracy. It might also have a salutary effect that extends throughout America's political life.

Formal, institutional reform in politics remains so unpredictable because governmental inertia overwhelmingly favors stasis over action. Incumbents fear change with any potential of jeopardizing their positions. Doing little or nothing, while always continuing to talk about reform, might seem hypocritical, but self-preservation prevails. Government is a slow-moving vehicle, inclined to frequent stops and detours down dead-end roads. By contrast, contemporary communications is in a frenetic state of constant motion, turning science fiction into fact with astonishing regularity. Among the array of emerging technologies, there are those leading to the promise of what's grandly called an "information superhighway" that journalists herald as being just around the corner. The political (and social) consequences of an interactive multi-media future will challenge tradition at every turn. To brave this new world will require a new kind of American citizen.

Back in 1938, after looking through "the peephole of science" and ruminating on a demonstration of an experimental means of communication, E. B. White wrote in *Harper's Magazine* ". . . I believe television is going to be the test of the modern world, and that in this new opportunity to see beyond the range of our vision we shall discover either a new and unbearable disturbance of the general peace or a saving radiance in the sky. We shall stand or fall by television—of that I am quite sure." Whether you view television as an "unbearable disturbance of the general peace or a saving radiance in the sky"—or something decidedly in between—is your own business. However, White's prediction that television would be "the test of the modern world" remains relevant and, in fact, assumes greater meaning as the medium becomes more dominant in different aspects of American life. That a household in the 1990s has a television going an average of almost seven hours each day tells just a portion of the story. How the medium is actually used—by people behind the screen and in front of it—creates the more demanding part of "the test."

Although statistics of viewership are high, what's being watched has dramatically changed in recent years. While the three major networks (ABC, CBS, NBC) commanded 92 percent of the combined audience share during the 1978–79 season, the percentage had dropped to 60 percent by 1992–93. Forecasters predict 45 percent or lower by the end of this decade. Network decline is occurring largely because other television sources are proliferating. In 1992, some seventy-six cable networks offered programming, with many more gearing up to join the crowd. Television specialization—"narrowcasting" in the argot of the business—mirrors what's been happening in radio and magazine publishing during the past several years. Instead of broadly casting a message to the public, people in communications target their work to slices or niches of the audience at large.

A wide-eyed pedestrian surveying several proposed blueprints for the information superhighway of the future can't be sure about its precise configuration. Free-market competition and government regulation will be critical determining factors. What's easy to see, though, is that the much-heralded highway ahead will make the past look like a country road, serviceable certainly but bumpy and unpaved in spots. Just over the horizon, different media and means of communication will merge into an interconnected, interlocking network of networks, with each appropriately outfitted household the intersection for messages of information, entertainment, commerce, and whatever else the highway can deliver. The coming together of the computer, television, cable, and telephone will create the possibility for receiving five-hundred TV channels, for interacting via electronic mail or video phone anywhere in the world, for shopping and banking from home, and for untold other services and pleasures. To focus on television, having the capability of personally programming whatever we want to see whenever we want to see it leads to talk of a "post-channel world" and the mind-boggling prospect of selecting something, from everything, to watch.

Political implications of this information-rich environment are profound. Should a citizen desire, it will be easy to follow a campaign or the status of a policy proposal by tuning in to television coverage of events or by calling up documents on the computer. Being politically informed, however, will require taking more personal initiative, because so many other media messages will be competing for our time and attention. From America's founding until quite recently, people in political life and civic-minded folk in general assumed, accurately or otherwise, that a body of public knowledge was shared in common by the citizenry at a given time. The relatively small number of information sources helped shape this belief. There were fewer distractions or alternatives. Now, with so much choice—and so much more to come—there will be new responsibilities of citizenship. Interestingly, with all the different possibilities for information, it will no longer serve much purpose to pillory "the media" for superficial or slanted coverage. Instead of criticizing, the public will be able to use the new technology to search out and find speeches, press conferences, town meetings, or debates so they can be watched for extended periods or in their entirety. To a certain extent, C-SPAN and CNN offer some of this possibility today, but this is the Wright Brothers' stage. Tomorrow promises greater access and the potential of more active citizen involvement.

Living in a world without interminable discussions of "media bias" might be a bleak prospect for certain commentators and intellectuals. However, most people who take advantage of their network of networks will discover everything they need to form their judgments and opinions. But an abundance of outlets do not an informed electorate make. Learning about political figures and issues will take work and time, with the process of receiving information involving deliberate personal selection. In addition, there will be less exposure to random political news because there will be less reliance on what we now have as network news programs, newspapers, and newsmagazines. Indeed, throughout communications today you find much hand-wringing and chin-pulling over the fate of these traditional forms of journalism. There's the nagging fear such forms and messages will go the way of smoke signals or carrier pigeons. In an interview when he retired from NBC News in 1993, John Chancellor remarked, "We have six institutions in the United States that are in grave danger: the three weekly newsmagazines and the three network news programs. Are we going to have another kind of extinction period like we had when *Collier's, Saturday Evening Post* and *Look* disappeared? My guess is we probably will by the end of this century."

Despite the demise of certain institutions, the amount of available news, analysis, and commentary will vastly increase in the future. Concerned citizens and political aficionados will be able to follow public figures and affairs as closely as they wish. With a flick of a switch and a few keyboard commands, local, state, and national coverage or information (like texts of statements or pending legislation) will appear. And there will always be more to view or consult because the information superhighway will offer a virtual infinity of political and governmental news—and everything else. The only limit will be on how much time a person wants to spend becoming informed.

Wondrously sunny as such an outlook might seem, clouds also loom on the horizon. Just as in biotechnology where scientific breakthroughs are accompanied by moral and scientific dilemmas, there are always unintended consequences in an environment of profound change, and questions arise. To what extent will an average American want detailed reports about the nation's political life? Will a person turn away from a vast smorgasbord of entertainment selections—new programs, old movies, sports at all hours—and myriad other possibilities—learning about cooking and home repair or corresponding with an electronic mail pen-pal in Paris—to follow what's happening in politics and government?

A five-hundred-channel receiver, operating along with a computer, tremendously broadens the scope of available messages; however, the level of audience fragmentation will be so great that a narrowing of the public mind could simultaneously occur. It will no longer be possible to take for granted that everyone knows certain information, and with so much competition (and clutter) within communications it's highly doubtful that collectively shared public moments—campaign debates, presidential speeches, major Congressional hearings—

will serve the purpose they once did when there were fewer options.

When each person is, indeed, an island of individually selected messages, the concept of a "public" becomes much less meaningful, and there is danger of divisiveness never before contemplated. Charles de Gaulle's chestnut about his beloved France—"How can you govern a country which has 246 varieties of cheese?"—is often quoted as a leader's lament of the difficulty of governing in a robustly varied democracy. Looking ahead, though, how will it be possible to rally a nation with five-hundred channels? Moreover, the notion of a "communications system," with certain qualities that foster unity among a diverse people, becomes absurd. There will be those, no doubt, who keep up with every political gyration. However, the number of people who are blissfully unaware of what's happening in public life can multiply, too, as they select other types of messages from their menus.

To a degree, this paradox of plentiful information and potential ignorance already exists. In *The Age of Missing Information*, Bill McKibben juxtaposes one day of watching all the programming on a ninety-three–channel cable system to a day spent out-of-doors amid nature. Early in the book, he writes: "We believe that we live in the 'age of information,' that there has been an information 'explosion,' an information 'revolution.' While in a certain narrow sense this is the case, in many important ways just the opposite is true. We also live at a moment of deep ignorance, when vital knowledge that humans have always possessed about who we are and where we live seems beyond our reach. An Unenlightenment. An age of missing information."[7]

McKibben's cautionary words take on greater meaning when the information superhighway comes into view. What can we expect in a communications environment of five-hundred channels and computer-linked gadgetry? To be fair to the future, it's possible that the opportunity of more selection will result in the public becoming more involved in matters of consequence that lead to better, enriched lives and to the making of "the good society." But such optimistic speculation requires a leap of faith that a down-to-earth realist isn't willing to take before there's more evidence. Motion sickness from information overload is just one potential side-effect from speeding along this freeway—or toll road.

Actually, the clouds of unanswered questions thicken as we look more deliberately at the horizon. There's the possibility that the cost for purchasing and using the new technology will, in effect, create a "communications underclass." The "hardware" won't be cheap, and subscribing to the "software" will be an on-going, monthly expense one's reluctant to compute. Those who can't take advantage of the information superhighway in their homes might be able to (if you will) hitchhike at a public library or school. Clearly, however, as democratic as the new media world might seem in theory, there will be "haves" and "have nots"—and the distance between them in the area of access will be greater than ever before. One wonders, too, whether free channels of communication will even exist, and what type of programming they might provide. Will such efforts be considered entitlements for those unable to afford the more expensive services? Will digitalization actually enhance democratization, or foster a data aristocracy?

Many of the articles in the popular press describing what the information superhighway will mean include the line (or close variation) that says, "Americans may never leave home again." Having user-friendly machines that reduce human contact or friendship might appeal to some people. But what will be the ultimate cost of such isolation? Somehow the prospect of "virtual reality" through technology replacing real reality seems depressing—and, frankly, anti-social. In such a world that promises working at home, shopping from home, being entertained and informed at home, life takes place at a remove, with a remote control quality rather than a hands-on feeling. Politically, it's difficult to imagine people with limited interpersonal experience being able to work out the compromises that frequently come from direct, (dare we say) human relationships. What kind of person, with what type of skills, will want to get involved in public life in the future?

Another critical concern involves exactly how people will use all these new technologies and all the messages they provide. More possibilities mean more choice, but there's the danger that comes from an overabundance of communications. Coping with so much can be intimidating and lead to following well-worn paths of personally preferred diversions—old sit-coms, music videos, travel programs, or non-stop soap operas. What will attract people is the great unknown, and the extent of user activity is a similarly large question mark. Can we really expect more interest in political life? Or less? In *The Future of the Mass Audience*, W. Russell Neuman surveys the high-tech landscape of "direct-broadcast satellites, personal computers, digital, high-definition, and inter-active television, videotex and teletext, electronic mail and high-speed-computer networks, as well as a variety of enhanced services for an expanding digital telephone network"[8] but concludes that tomorrow won't be all that different from today. As he notes much later in his methodical exposition and analysis:

> . . . commentaries on interactivity have been, on the whole, quite sanguine. Although not revolutionary or

deterministic in effect, the prospects for increased
control over the communications process will, at the
very least, allow those who are so inclined to draw
more information and enjoyment from the media
around them. There is, however, a significant qualifi-
cation, and it is a central theme of this book: The
reality is likely to fall far short of the potential. The
lesson from the mass psychology of media behavior is
that learning is partial, for the learner is selective and
semiattentive. The mass citizenry, for most issues,
simply will not take the time to learn more or understand more deeply, no matter how inexpensive or
convenient such further learning may be.[9]

Probing and insightful as Neuman is, he avoids consideration of circumstances and forces that could disrupt
the political media environment and make it different
from what he foresees as the continuation of the existing
pattern. If the election year of 1992 taught no other
lesson, it is that people can be motivated to be more
attentive and active when they sense the stakes are high
and their involvement matters. Throughout the campaign, traditional ways of communicating (speeches, press
conferences, debates, commercials) merged with newer
forms (talk shows, town meetings, satellite-delivered local
interviews, infomercials) to create a political climate
unlike any ever before. There were more opportunities
for interaction between the politicians and the citizens.
Many of the messages had a two-way quality—they were
responses to the public's questions—rather than the usual
one-way arrangement of speaking to an audience of
potential voters.

In the wake of 1992, citizen interaction has continued
to develop and become more prominent in American
political life. What's currently happening bears close

scrutiny because the emerging technology of the future will greatly expand participatory possibilities, either directly or indirectly. Take, for example, the phenomenon of talk radio. In 1993, there were over 600 different talk shows on the air, with 1,000 (of the nation's 10,000 stations) devoted primarily to a talk format. Discussing politics and government on every level occupies a large chunk of talk-show time. Rush Limbaugh is fond of telling his listeners (over sixteen-million people on over 600 stations, according to a mid-1993 *Wall Street Journal* profile), "Everything I do here has a political point." Limbaugh is not alone—just hugely more successful than others in his trade. By cleverly combining information and entertainment, he appeals to people who might not even agree with his political perspective. And for those who are in agreement, fan loyalty approaches a transcendental experience.

Signs proclaiming "Rush is God" reflect a Second-Coming allegiance some observers rightly find unsettling. However, the response to his work in radio signifies considerable public interest in public affairs and a desire by a large number of citizens to voice their opinions about political and government matters. Expressing such views takes several forms, including calls to the program and messages to people in public life. Effective as Limbaugh might be in acquainting millions with certain aspects of political life—and his radio program is merely one dimension of a multi-media life encompassing a television show, a monthly newsletter, best-selling books, and speeches—he symbolizes a potential danger to democracy, especially in terms of the future.

During the summer of 1993, an unnamed official in the Clinton administration told *U.S. News & World Report* for a cover story on Limbaugh, "The Mouth That Roars," "We're wired in real time now. People hear something and immediately react without reflection, without comparing what Rush Limbaugh says to, say, what Dan Rather says. They can wing in with faxes and telegrams and calls based only on Limbaugh, and for many he is the sole source of information." That people want to let elected officials know what they're thinking is laudable. But to what extent is the thinking theirs or someone else's, and how much different is the response generated by talk shows from efforts of political influence engineered by, for instance, the National Rifle Association? There's a chance that an angry blast of reaction will lead to a counterreaction, without the time necessary for deliberation.

The American system of democracy, complete with three branches of government with their check and balances, was designed to avoid being overly rushed in making public decisions. Let passions cool, the Founders thought. Talk shows and other forms of contemporary communications bring subjects into focus quickly and accelerate the process in ways that provoke concern. For instance, shortly after Clinton's inauguration, Federal Judge Kimba Wood withdrew as a possible nominee for Attorney General, and a principal reason cited was White House fear of a talk-show campaign against her similar to the one that contributed to Zoë Baird's withdrawal just days before as a candidate for the same position. (Both women had employed illegal aliens for child care, but Wood vowed she could prove she had not violated the law). The cases were different, and an argument can be made that Wood wasn't given a real chance to have her say. Worry over the talk-show mobilized mob was enough to determine her fate, and that in itself is troubling. To be sure, having public officials who are out-of-touch is anti-democratic and undesirable. (A headline in *The Washington Post* on January 15, 1993 announced "Baird's Hiring Disclosure Not Seen as Major Block," but a week later she withdrew.) However, fear of talk-show sound and fury is not desirable either, particularly if that fear results in hurried overreaction. In the years to come, people in political life will have to learn to deal with the angry, immediate messages more deliberately to avoid momentary (and, in many cases, emotional) blasts of political rage.

Talk-show provocation for the public to communicate with elected officials is just one method of citizen feedback that exists today and could become larger (and more influential) in the future. The Clinton Administration, in fact, has experimented with the new technology to set up never-before-tried ways of delivering and receiving messages. Using electronic mail, computer services, and voice mail, the White House is able to send out speeches, proclamations, and other announcements, while citizens (with appropriate access) can say what's on their minds in return. According to news reports, the volume of incoming messages is higher than it's ever been. A tomorrow that promises greater ease for such communication could well mean that future presidents will be on the receiving end of considerably more than the daily average of 75,850 messages that was computed in 1993. Dealing effectively with such volume will be difficult, if not impossible, but (except for interest-group or other single-issue campaigns) some sense of the public mood and citizen concern can emerge. These messages have similar relevance as survey research, although surveys, of course, are more scientific and representative. These messages should be treated as advisory information for an elected official, who is trying to lead while remaining in touch with popular opinion. But making decisions based on this new linkage between the government and the governed would be chancy governance, because a different viewpoint could quickly replace an earlier one and result in policy inconsistency and administrative instability. In a climate of accelerated availability of information, American democracy has to foster means of deceleration that contribute to purposeful action. This doesn't mean turning a deaf-ear (or blind-eye) to huge numbers of incoming messages. Rather, it means being sensitive to public opinion while conducting statecraft that has direction and resolve.

The Clinton Administration's use of various means of new communications technology is part of a more comprehensive strategy for connecting with the public. What you see happening today is simultaneously a flashback to the 1992 campaign and a preview of political communication to come in years ahead. The president and the people around him emphasize getting out their message via locally based outlets and in nationally delivered forums that provide greater contact with the public at large. By the time of Clinton's first, official East Room press conference (on March 23, 1993), he had conducted some twenty-five meetings with local journalists. The strategy of stiffing the White House press corps changed later that spring, especially with the arrival of Washington-insider David Gergen to the Clinton staff. Over time there developed the realization that the traditional ways of presidential communication could not be abandoned without enduring continuing criticism from mainstream, national sources (broadcast networks, wire services, large newspapers, and newsmagazines).

The greater availability for the elite, establishment media augmented the original White House approach. Stressing local and "new news" opportunities remained at the center of the Clinton effort to relate with the public via popular forms of communication. For instance, about two-hundred radio talk-show hosts from around the country came to the White House in September 1993 for a briefing on the administration's health care pro-

gram, and some sixty later conducted their local programs directly from the White House lawn. Clinton
continued to take part in regional and national town
meetings that featured citizens quizzing the president on
domestic and international affairs. In the fall of 1993,
Vice President Al Gore, the leader of the administration's
project for "reinventing government," talked about his
plan with the Washington press, but then headed to New
York for appearances on "Donahue" and the "Late Show"
with David Letterman. As the vice president left the set
of Letterman's program, the host-comedian wished him
"good luck with this government thing," leading Eliza-
beth Kolbert of *The New York Times* to observe: "It was
Mr. Gore's appearance on Mr. Letterman's show, though,
that seemed finally to merge politics and entertainment
into one funny, knowing and thoroughly sarcastic package." Possibly; but the appearance (which included
jocular banter and the vice president attempting to break
a government-issue ashtray with a hammer) also delivered the administration's thinking to a large audience
that might not pay much attention to news, and made a
politician, perceived as stiff and somewhat humorless,
more appealing as a personality.

   Targeting messages for delivery by local outlets and
the "new news" is shrewd for several reasons. Research
about television reveals that most people prefer local
news to network fare, and there has been an explosion
of local news programming in recent years. Some cities
(New York, Chicago, Washington, to name a few) have
cable channels devoted exclusively to local news around-
the-clock, and elsewhere the amount of available time to
fill makes an interview with the president (or any other
high administration officials) a welcome addition to any
program. Moreover, local journalists, both broadcast and
print, tend to ask less barbed or accusatory questions.

It's a less combative atmosphere than an exchange with Washington reporters.

Clinton's communications strategy is a variation of the late Tip O'Neill's maxim that "all politics is local." In addition, the "new news" formats help create connections between public officials and the public in untraditional settings that, in most cases, allow these public officials greater control in delivering their message. With so many media sources and so much fragmentation, maintaining focus on an issue is difficult but essential. In future years, it will be even harder to capture the public's attention because there will be vastly more competition. To a degree, the Clinton approach foreshadows what we can expect. As Sidney Blumenthal observed in *The New Yorker* in 1993, "What the President seeks is unmediated communication." Unmediated communication means direct delivery to the citizenry—and connection within a controlled environment. The new technology and new formats will expand these opportunities as the information superhighway becomes reality.

Burgeoning media capabilities set minds to wondering about establishing stronger links between those governing and the governed. As Bruce Reed, one of Clinton's top advisers, told a newspaper reporter in 1993: "I think the world of news has changed over the last few years. I think the progress in technology combined with political failure in Washington now has made direct democracy both possible and necessary." Reed's statement is just one of many advocating interactivity by the citizenry in some form of "teledemocracy." Part of Ross Perot's appeal in 1992 and afterwards can be traced to his proposal for creating "electronic town halls." Originally conceived in 1969, Perot's plan entails presentations of differing viewpoints, public reaction to the options through a push-button device on the television or via a touch-tone phone, and tabulation of the results by congressional district or state. Then members of the House and Senate would be given these figures prior to legislative votes related to the subject. Perot told interviewers from *TV Guide* in 1992, "It's the old town-hall meeting, expanded, using modern technology. It's what happens when people used to come together in a little village and discuss and debate what needed to be done, and reach a consensus and do it. People then send a laser-like message to their government giving their opinion. It is democracy in its purest form."

Purity, however, is in the eye of the beholder, and establishment of a system of teledemocracy runs the risk of opening a Pandora's box with ominous consequences for the future. Instead of being a representative democracy, America would be moving to—if not actually become— a plebiscitary democracy. As romantic or seductive as that prospect might sound to some, serious questions abound. How binding would the "electronic town-hall" results be on lawmakers? What impact would there be on a legislator for *not* voting with the majority of teledemocrats? How many different measures would be dealt with in the town-hall format? Would the approach be used on the state and local levels as well as the national? Besides such concerns, the type of presentation and the level of participation are worrisome. Television is a visual medium better at conveying emotion than information, and it is particularly successful in projecting someone's personality.

What the sides could show in their presentations, and who might speak on behalf of each side would be important, if not critical. For instance, say rampant starvation is plaguing an African country, and thousands are dying, including children. What if the possibility of a humanitarian military mission is the topic of an electronic town-hall meeting, and video footage of the conditions could be aired? It's difficult to imagine anything less than resounding support. But say a few weeks or months later circumstances change, and American forces engage in some fighting to protect themselves and their work. Some soldiers are killed or captured, a few even dragged through the streets—with television showing these scenes. And what if an electronic town-hall session is scheduled to debate whether to withdraw the American forces immediately, and some of the TV coverage can be shown? You get the picture.

How the people vote might make the most sense and be the wisest policy, but such decisions could be driven by pictures to a much greater extent than we see today with government officials. In addition, it's legitimate to wonder how complicated or unpopular-but-necessary domestic matters would be handled in an electronic town-hall setting. The intricacies of a new national health care program (to take one striking example) would be difficult to present—and that is glaring understatement. The tele-democratic response would efficiently count those in favor and those opposed, but missing in such a system would be various points of compromise that might refine the program and correct problems.

Questions about public participation flow from those about format. Who would become involved in this new plebiscitary system? Would people without the means to afford the new technology be excluded? Is it reasonable to expect vast numbers of Americans to take the required time to render informed judgments on a regular basis? Would activist groups, committed to certain causes, exert themselves to swing a vote one way or another? Such concerns no doubt offend a teledemocrat or town-hall proponent, but they are real and worth pondering. It should be stressed that Perot's proposal is just one of many offered in recent years, as communication systems have become more sophisticated. Books—such as Richard Hollander's *Video Democracy: The Vote-from-Home Revolution* and Ted Wachtel's *The Electronic Congress: A Blueprint for Participatory Democracy*—sketch out specific plans, and groups across the country are advocating measures for greater citizen involvement.[10]

The information superhighway will make interactivity or two-way communication not only possible but commonplace. However, that the technology exists doesn't mean it should be used in a way that changes the basic character of the American system. If people in communications—and *not* government—want to design town-hall occasions, which include public officials taking sides, and there's a chance for viewers to register their views at the end, then education of the citizenry might be well served. The response would be informal, akin to a public opinion poll. No problem. It's the formal nature of teledemocracy or the undue pressure from teleplebiscite-after-teleplebiscite that makes the future potentially dangerous.

One fear would be that, like most things in communications, the electronic town hall might be a short-term novelty, a fad involving fewer and fewer people over time. If that happened, special interests could easily mobilize and show their muscle. Then what would be accomplished? *New York Times* columnist Russell Baker takes a different yet related approach to the question of interaction: "Speaking of the wonderful new information age when, they now tell us, we'll be able to 'talk back' to our television sets, what makes them think we have anything to say to our television sets? The purpose of television is to spare people with nothing on their minds the necessity of making conversation, isn't it? Who wants to live in a world where millions of people with nothing on their minds sit around struggling to think of something interesting enough to say to their television sets?"

In the context of serious political issues, Baker's musing might seem overly wry, tongue too much in cheek. His point, however, has merit in that the "talk back" phenomenon could ultimately be less representative—and more undemocratic—than the situation that exists today. Using the new communication technology in all of its variety to enhance American democracy should be a primary objective for public officials and for the public at large in the years ahead. More sophisticated and instantaneous means of presenting ideas, voicing opinions, and registering complaints will be able to reduce the distance between government and the governed. However, taking advantage of these new, high-tech possibilities doesn't mean taking a step into a vast unknown world, where citizens are deciding day-to-day matters of governance with the click of a remote-control button.

In *The Medium is the Massage*, Marshall McLuhan playfully pontificates, "We look at the present through a rear-view mirror. We march backwards into the future."[11] The quirky theorist of mid-twentieth–century communications technology is, in his way, suggesting a phenomenon we see around us today, one that will take on more profound significance in the years to come. The abundance of new media possibilities is destroying the concept of the "mass audience" and "mass communication." Equipped with everything from a goggle-like headset (called "Virtual Vision") that allows television watching while walking or attending an event, to portable fax machines, to ready access to the Internet web of over 11,000 computer networks reaching millions of users in countries across the globe, we march backwards, away from "the mass," to a future that will demand nineteenth-century American values: self-reliance and individualism within a framework of community.

Having an interactive multimedia network of networks widely available gives new meaning to the word "narrowcasting," and, somewhat paradoxically, television's dominance will decline because there will be so many different options undercutting the influence of all the other competing messages. Instead of considering television as a cultural, social, and political force—with the word "force" deliberately in the singular—the wealth of new options will make the medium closer to a common language, with each viewer having his or her distinct way of talking. This view, however, implies that someone has something to say. Back in the seventeenth century in one of his *Pensées*, Pascal remarked that "all the unhappiness of man arises from one thing only, namely that he is incapable of abiding quietly in one room." To what extent will a room, even furnished with a machine that receives five-hundred channels and other types of communication, be different from one in the past? Will so much choice lead to greater personal happiness or to bewilderment? Will people be actively engaged or remain relatively passive?

In the specific context of political life, it's already clear that the individual citizen will have to assume new obligations and responsibilities in carrying out civic duties. There will be a wealth of messages available via the information superhighway, but acquiring the necessary knowledge to make judgments about politics and government will take much greater personal effort. Despite the vastly different time and political communications environment, Lincoln's memorable words from his message to Congress in 1862 aptly pertain to what Americans will face in the future: "The dogmas of the quiet past are inadequate to the stormy present. . . . As our case is new, so we must think anew, and act anew."

To think and act anew is the dual challenge citizens face. The interaction between public figures and the public that has taken place through the media as a result of everything that happened in 1992 demonstrates the clear desire to become more directly involved. More and more, the people want to ask questions and to receive their own responses—rather than rely on journalists, with their agendas, to serve as intermediaries. Such public involvement strengthens democracy by making the citizenry more central to political life. The shift from relative passivity to appreciable activity we currently see is a sign of civic concern that the prospect of increased media interactivity can foster and enhance.

If used effectively, the emerging communications technology will create greater accountability—without undermining the foundations of the American system of representative democracy. When Gerald Ford became president after Richard Nixon's resignation, he said, "Here the people rule." How the people rule in the future will be shaped to a considerable degree by the ways they work with—and rule—the different, stunningly numerous media possibilities that will be available. The question for today, and tomorrow, is: Will Americans make time for politics and government, as they maneuver through the heavy traffic on the information superhighway? With so many other media diversions competing for someone's time and attention, it won't be easy. But democracy has never been easy—nor should it be. Even in a world where "artificial intelligence" and "virtual reality" are common, "virtual democracy" has no place.

As we move into the twenty-first century, who will create the citizenry of the United States? What can we expect the American public of the future to look like? The diverse means of communications will be available to a polity that itself is increasingly diverse. Indeed, debates about "multiculturalism" and "diversity," which have reverberated for the past decade, are the prelude to demographic changes of such profound potential consequence that someone looking back at America in 1950 and also looking forward to the U.S. in 2050 might claim no country's population can shift so dramatically in a century's time. However, since the founding of the nation, history and myth offer a similar lesson: Here anything is possible.

To intrude some statistics, the census of 1950 revealed this composition of the American people:

TOTAL	150,697,361
White	134,942,028
Negro	15,042,286
Indian	343,410
Japanese	141,768
Chinese	117,629
All Other	110,240

Using the Census Bureau's classifications for the people counted in 1950, the percentages were 89.5 "White" (82.8% "native" and 6.7% "foreign born"), 10.0 "Negro," and 0.5 "Other races."[12]

Although there were some changes in the make-up of the populace between 1950 and 1980, the decade from 1980 until 1990 is critical to understanding what will be happening during the coming years. Estimates vary, but approximately 11 million people immigrated to the United States in the 1980s, 9 million legally and 2 million illegally. This influx of immigrants to this nation of immigrants set a record for a ten-year period, with those of Hispanic and Asian heritage leading the way. Comparing the population figures for 1980 and 1990 is revealing. As Ronald Takaki, the historian and leader of the multicultural studies movement, notes: "The new face of America has a darker hue."[13]

RESIDENT POPULATION DISTRIBUTION FOR THE UNITED STATES:[14] 1980 and 1990

	1980		1990		
	Number	%	Number	%	Change
TOTAL population	226,545,805	100.0	248,709,873	100.0	9.8
White	188,371,622	83.1	199,686,070	80.3	6.0
Black	26,495,020	11.7	29,986,060	12.1	13.2
Hispanic origin	14,608,673	6.4	22,354,059	9.0	53.0
American Indian, Eskimo or Aleut	1,420,400	0.6	1,959,234	0.8	37.9
Asian or Pacific Islander	3,500,439	1.5	7,273,662	2.9	107.8
Other race	6,758,319	3.0	9,804,847	3.9	45.1

Projections by the Bureau of the Census reflect much greater acceleration in these current trends. Forecasts in recent years provide changing sets of numbers as new data become factors for analysis, but the statistical conclusions announced in late 1993 give an indication of what we can expect in the twenty-first century.

PROJECTED POPULATION DISTRIBUTION[15]

Year: 2000

TOTAL Population	276,241,000	100.0%
White	197,872,000	71.6%
Black	33,741,000	12.2%
American Indian	2,055,000	0.7%
Asian	11,407,000	4.1%
Hispanic Origin	31,166,000	11.3%

Year: 2020

TOTAL Population	325,942,000	100.0%
White	208,280,000	63.9%
Black	42,459,000	13.0%
American Indian	2,641,000	0.8%
Asian	21,345,000	6.5%
Hispanic Origin	51,217,000	15.7%

Year: 2050

TOTAL Population	392,031,000	100.0%
White	205,849,000	52.5%
Black	56,346,000	14.4%
American Indian	3,701,000	0.9%
Asian	38,064,000	9.7%
Hispanic Origin	88,071,000	22.5%

What do these predictions mean for American political life in the future? Clearly, the dominance of people classified as "non-Hispanic white" will be much less pronounced during the next century. This fact will be particularly true and potentially significant in certain states—notably California, New York, Texas, Florida,

New Jersey, Illinois, and Massachusetts. These seven states, according to a study conducted by the Population Studies Center at the University of Michigan, have received over two-thirds of the recent immigrants to the United States. One phenomenon that is occurring simultaneously with all of the new arrivals is the departure of "non-Hispanic whites" from these same states. Demographers see parallels between earlier patterns of movement, where whites left certain cities and particular neighborhoods to go to the suburbs, and what's currently happening. The scale, however, is larger, affecting entire states and regions, with the case of California especially illustrative. As the tide of immigration kept rising, the state's economic fortunes began to fall. The scramble for jobs became so intense that millions of white Californians moved to Nevada, Arizona, Washington, and Oregon—making these states more decidedly white in their composition. It's predicted that California, which in 1993 had a population that was 56 percent non-Hispanic white, will see its make-up change to less than half white within a decade.

As the non-Hispanic white dominance declines, political activity by African Americans, Asian Americans, and Hispanic Americans will without question pick up and be particularly powerful in specific areas. Just how quickly this might happen is an open question. In California, for example, the 1990 census counted 2.9 million Asian Americans and 7.7 million Hispanics, but the most recent study of voting records show 750,000 Asian Americans and 1.5 million Hispanics actually registered to vote. Be that as it may, there's little doubt that groups such as the Congressional Black Caucus and the Congressional Hispanic Caucus will gain greater clout in Washington, as their numbers increase.

And, of course, in terms of active political involvement changes are by no means just related to race and ethnicity. Gender is also critical. One of the consequences of the women's movement is the growing number of female candidates vying for political office on all levels of government. In the House of Representatives, for example, a total of 108 women competed in the general election of 1992, with 47 victorious. The previous Congress had 28 women. On the Senate side, the number of women serving jumped from two in 1992 to seven in 1993, with both of California's Senate seats being contested in 1992 won by women and Carol Moseley-Braun of Illinois becoming the first African-American woman in the chamber. In state legislatures across the country, women now occupy over 20 percent of the offices, and on the mayoral level nationally the total is just under 20 percent.

Combine the ethnic and racial changes with the emergence of women as active participants and American political life of tomorrow will, at first glance, look very different from what we have seen in the past. However, of vastly more importance than the appearance will be the extent to which Americans in the future retain and cultivate the values, ideals, and beliefs that form our democratic heritage. With so much diversity within the U.S. population, the dangers that come from divisions multiply. Demographic dilemmas can take the place of Walt Whitman's "democratic vistas." If divisions develop, become pronounced, and persist, maintaining national unity or a sense of the common good is difficult, if not impossible. And, with the available communications so pluralistic, the media don't provide much in the way of cohesion. In fact, with the coming of the information superhighway, a case could be made that the existence of the multi-media environment exacerbates the situation and contributes to the problem of fragmentation.

Fear about a future that emphasizes differences rather than similarities helps animate the thinking of people who criticize the more extreme advocates of multiculturalism. Several liberal intellectuals (notably Arthur M. Schlesinger, Jr., C. Vann Woodward, Alfred Kazin, Irving Howe) have written and spoken as forcefully as such noted conservatives as William Bennett, George Will, Diane Ravitch, and Russell Kirk to warn that any semblance of unity is threatened if specific groups go their way and disregard the interests of the whole society. In *The Disuniting of America: Reflections on a Multicultural Society*, Schlesinger writes:

> The ethnicity rage in general and Afrocentricity in particular not only divert attention from the real needs but exacerbate the problems. The recent apotheosis of ethnicity, black, brown, red, yellow, white, has revived the dismal prospect that in happy melting-pot days Americans thought the republic was moving safely beyond—that is, a society fragmented into separate ethnic communities. The cult of ethnicity exaggerates differences, intensifies resentments and antagonisms, drives ever deeper the awful wedges between races and nationalities. The endgame is self-pity and self-ghettoization.[16]

Schlesinger, who at the mid-point of the twentieth century eloquently argued in *The Vital Center* for a new American politics based on freedom, continues to see the need for a center that holds the country together. Near the end of *The Disuniting of America*, he states:

> The genius of America lies in its capacity to forge a single nation from peoples of remarkably diverse racial, religious, and ethnic origins. It has done so because democratic principles provide both the philosophical bond of union and practical experience in civic participation. The American Creed envisages a nation composed of individuals making their own

choices and accountable to themselves, not a nation
based on inviolable ethnic communities. The Constitution turns on individual rights, not on group rights.
Law, in order to rectify past wrongs, has from time to
time (and in my view often properly so) acknowledged
the claims of groups; but this is the exception, not the
rule.[17]

Persuasive as Schlesinger's book might be in its appeal
for unity, the strength of forces pulling in opposite directions will intensify in future years, presenting colossal
challenges to American political life. It's not only a matter
of diversity in the population. (The 1990 census revealed
that 329 languages were spoken by citizens in the United
States, and there was criticism that there weren't enough
categories to offer an accurate profile of the country's
composition.) Institutions that previously served as in-
struments of cohesion now seem to have much less
power to serve that function. This is seen already, to varying degrees, with religion, education, business, industry,
and civic organizations. As Colorado Governor Roy
Romer told David Broder of *The Washington Post* in
1993 about the proposals for changing educational funding in a number of states, "When it's no longer possible
for a kid to be safe or be educated in a public school, you
have to let the family pull out. But before we give up on
it, we ought to remember what the public school has
meant to us—as the meeting ground for all kinds of
Americans. When you encourage separate schools for
Methodists, for Catholics, for Lutherans, when you
divide youngsters by race or class or by their parents'
view of Creation, you become less like America—and
more like Bosnia. We ought to be careful where we go."
    Two other institutions that are in the process of rede-
fining themselves—and critical to our future democratic
life—are the political parties and the major, mainstream

media with national reach and impact. As the Democratic and Republican parties have lost the clout they once had, "special" or "single interest" organizations and political action committees have gained influence—and to a troubling extent. Historically, what a party favors and supports is less narrow and more inclusive than a proposal from a specific group with a definite agenda. In communications, the concept of "mass" is *passé*, as the possibilities for personally choosing your information and entertainment multiply. With so many different messages competing for our time and attention, what events or stories available to the media will serve as the connective tissue or cement in the future? Will a president's inaugural address or ceremonial funeral, a walk on the moon or a political debate, a celebration of a national anniversary or coverage of a military operation continue to be a widely shared, public experience in such a diverse communications environment?

As institutional and technological forces pull people every which way, political figures will have to find ways to establish and maintain the citizen's focus on significant issues and concerns, things that matter to security, welfare, exercising rights, and—yes—the common good. To fail to do this will result not only in an acceleration of fragmentation—imagine countless atoms without a nucleus—but in an absence of collective public purpose to tackle complicated problems affecting the populace as a whole. In *Democracy in America*, Alexis de Tocqueville rhapsodizes about what he encountered in Jacksonian America of the nineteenth century: "Millions of men are all marching together toward the same point on the horizon; their languages, religions, and mores are different, but they have one common aim. They have been told that fortune is to be found somewhere toward the west, and they hasten to seek it."[18]

Tocqueville, of course, sees "fortune" as encompassing private gain in a capitalistic, free-market economy as well as democratic virtues of American citizenship. However, the "one common aim" is the point to stress. Given what's happening and will happen, will the civil religion that Tocqueville celebrated continue to be a prime agent for cohesion, linking all citizens regardless of their particular characteristics and individual interests? Without a commonality of aim, what can we realistically expect for the nation's trajectory during the twenty-first century?

In looking forward to fathom the future and the questions it provokes, it's valuable to look backward to consider what's shaped and propelled America since its founding. Democratic values and ideals—freedom, equality, justice, openness, tolerance—coagulate to form the lifeblood of the nation. Political, governmental, and civic activity channel the flow and provide direction. Such activities will be more difficult but no less essential in years to come. Even at a time when the public square is replaced by a multi-media personal computer, American political life can—and should—create the necessary connections among a diverse citizenry.

Early in this country's history, President Thomas Jefferson wrote in a letter, "No experiment can be more interesting than that we are now trying, and which we trust will end in establishing the fact that man may be governed by reason and truth. Our first object should therefore be, to leave open to him all the avenues of truth." The experiment continues, with men and women of all ages and backgrounds involved and with a multitude of avenues of truth available. Governing ourselves tomorrow, with whatever reason and wisdom can be summoned, will mean what it does today: Demanding democracy—and responding to democracy's demands.

Notes

Introduction

1. Everette E. Dennis, Wendy Zeligson Adler, Martha FitzSimon, John Pavlik, Edward C. Pease, Dirk Smillie, and Mark Thalhimer, *The Homestretch: New Politics. New Media. New Voters?* (New York: Freedom Forum Media Studies Center, 1992), p. 99.

2. George F. Kennan, *Around the Cragged Hill: A Personal and Political Philosophy* (New York: W. W. Norton, 1993), p. 63.

3. For a discussion of the changes in the primaries and caucuses, see the chapter "Smokeless Politics" in Robert Schmuhl, *Statecraft and Stagecraft: American Political Life in the Age of Personality* (Notre Dame, Ind.: University of Notre Dame Press, 1990).

4. Kevin Phillips, *Boiling Point: Democrats, Republicans, and the Decline of Middle-Class Prosperity* (New York: Random House, 1993), p. 258.

Looking Backward

1. Donald L. Barlett and James B. Steele, *America: What Went Wrong?* (Kansas City: Andrews and McMeel, 1992), p. 191.

2. Everette E. Dennis, Martha FitzSimon, John Pavlik, Seth Rachlin, Dirk Smillie, David Stebenne, and Mark Thal-

himer, *Covering the Presidential Primaries* (New York: Freedom Forum Media Studies Center, 1992), p. 28.

3. Ibid., p. 13.

4. Tom Rosenstiel, *Strange Bedfellows: How Television and the Presidential Candidates Changed American Politics, 1992* (New York: Hyperion, 1993), p. 64.

5. Larry J. Sabato, *Feeding Frenzy: How Attack Journalism Has Transformed American Politics* (New York: Free Press, 1991), pp. 220–221.

6. Larry King, with Mark Stencel, *On the Line: The New Road to the White House* (New York: Harcourt Brace and Company, 1993), p. 6.

7. John Updike, *Rabbit at Rest* (New York: Alfred A. Knopf, 1990), p. 295.

8. Richard Ben Cramer, *What It Takes: The Way to the White House* (New York: Random House, 1992), p. 415.

9. Ibid., p. 797. Ellipses and emphasis in original.

10. Ibid., p. 154.

11. See Arthur M. Schlesinger, Jr., *The Cycles of American History* (Boston: Houghton Mifflin Company, 1986).

12. Gore Vidal, *United States: Essays 1952–1992* (New York: Random House, 1993), p. 831.

13. E. J. Dionne, Jr., *Why Americans Hate Politics* (New York: Simon and Schuster, 1991), p. 355.

14. Rosenstiel, *Strange Bedfellows*, pp. 79–80.

15. See the chapter "Blowing the Whistle" in Jack W. Germond and Jules Witcover, *Mad as Hell: Revolt at the Ballot Box, 1992* (New York: Warner Books, 1993).

16. Dennis, et al., *The Homestretch*, p. 87.

17. Nielsen Media Research, *Nielsen Tunes in to Politics: Tracking the Presidential Election Years (1960–1992)* (New York: Nielsen Media Research, 1993), p. 10.

18. Bruce Buchanan, *The Markle Commission on the Media and the Electorate: Key Findings* (New York: John and Mary R. Markle Foundation, 1990), p. 22.

19. Samuel L. Popkin, *The Reasoning Voter: Communication and Persuasion in Presidential Campaigns* (Chicago: University of Chicago Press, 1991), p. 43.

20. Phillips, *Boiling Point*, p. 245.

21. Gil Troy, *See How They Ran: The Changing Role of the Presidential Candidate* (New York: Free Press, 1991), p. 204.

Looking Forward

1. Michael R. Beschloss and Strobe Talbott, *At the Highest Levels: The Inside Story of the End of the Cold War* (Boston: Little, Brown and Company, 1993), pp. 3–4.

2. Paul Taylor, "Political Coverage in the 1990s: Teaching the Old News New Tricks," in *The New News v. The Old News: The Press and Politics in the 1990s*, ed. Suzanne Charlé (New York: Twentieth Century Fund Press, 1992), p. 61.

3. Stephen Bates, *The Future of Presidential Debates* (Washington, D.C.: Annenberg Washington Program, 1993), p. 10.

4. Newton N. Minow, *Annenberg Washington Program Annual Report, 1992–1993* (Washington, D.C.: Annenberg Washington Program, 1993), p. 10.

5. For a discussion of alternative approaches to the current nominating system, see the chapter "Smokeless Politics" in Schmuhl, *Statecraft and Stagecraft.*

6. Gene Shalit and Lawrence K. Grossman, eds., *Somehow It Works: A Candid Portrait of the 1964 Presidential Election by NBC News* (Garden City, N.Y.: Doubleday, 1965).

7. Bill McKibben, *The Age of Missing Information* (New York: Random House, 1992), p. 9.

8. W. Russell Neuman, *The Future of the Mass Audience* (Cambridge: Cambridge University Press, 1991), pp. ix–x.

9. Ibid., p. 109.

10. See Richard Hollander, *Video Democracy: The Vote-from-Home Revolution* (Mount Airy, Md.: Lomond Publications, 1985) and Ted Wachtel, *The Electronic Congress: A*

Blueprint for Participatory Democracy (Pipersville, Penn.: Piper's Press, 1992).

11. Marshall McLuhan, with Quentin Fiore, *The Medium is the Massage: An Inventory of Effects* (New York: Bantam Books, 1967), p. 75.

12. Bureau of the Census, *Census of Population: 1950*, Vol. II of *Characteristics of the Population*, Part I of *United States Summary* (Washington, D.C.: U.S. Government Printing Office, 1953), p. 1:88, table 36.

13. Ronald Takaki, *From Different Shores: Perspectives on Race and Ethnicity in America*, ed. Ronald Takaki (New York: Oxford University Press, 1987), p. 5. See also Ronald Takaki, *A Different Mirror: A History of Multicultural America* (Boston: Little, Brown and Company, 1993).

14. George Brown Tindall and Daniel E. Shi, *America: A Narrative History*, 3rd ed. (New York: W. W. Norton, 1993), p. 1000.

15. See Bureau of the Census, *Population Projections of the United States, by Age, Sex, Race, and Hispanic Origin: 1993 to 2050* (Washington, D.C.: U.S. Government Printing Office, 1993).

16. Arthur M. Schlesinger, Jr., *The Disuniting of America: Reflections on a Multicultural Society* (New York: W. W. Norton, 1992), p. 102.

17. Ibid., p. 134.

18. Alexis de Tocqueville, *Democracy in America*, trans. George Lawrence, ed. J. P. Mayer and Max Lerner (New York: Harper & Row, 1966), p. 259.

Acknowledgments and Annotations

Some sections of this book originally appeared, in much different form, in articles for the *Chicago Tribune, The Philadelphia Inquirer, USA Today*, and *Notre Dame Magazine*. I'm grateful to the editors with whom I worked—F. Richard Ciccone and Dianne Donovan at the *Tribune*, Mike Leary at *The Inquirer*, Sid Hurlburt at *USA Today*, and Walt Collins at *Notre Dame Magazine*— for permission to adapt material in their pages for these pages.

I'm also grateful to Richard C. Phalen and his publisher, Diamond Communications, for their permission to use passages from the chapter I contributed to the oral history, *In Our Time: Rediscovering America— 1940–1990s*, which appeared in 1993. Some of the points about demographic change in America that appear near the end of the section "Looking Forward" come from a paper, "America and Multiculturalism," which was presented at the Fulbright Colloquium on "Citizenship and Rights in Multicultural Societies." The Colloquium took place in Bologna, Italy, April 15–17, 1993, and support from the Fulbright Commission and the Institute for Scholarship in the Liberal Arts of the University of Notre Dame made the completion and presentation of the paper possible.

Looking back through my notebooks for 1992 and early 1993, I tally jottings that add up to well over a hundred interviews for newspapers, magazines, and broadcast outlets of one kind or another. I don't report the number to brag—on several occasions little or nothing was actually used—but to make the point that writing this book allowed me (in the phrase heard so often on the floor of Congress) "to revise and extend my remarks." In preparing for interviews or directly afterwards, I'd scribble notebook entries about the specific topic under consideration. As a result, much of the "Looking Backward" section draws on running commentary composed during the campaign that's now presented (I hope) with some thematic coherence.

James Langford, Director of the University of Notre Dame Press, deserves more than a word of thanks. We've worked together on four books now, and he is an invaluable source of advice and encouragement. An author is not only grateful but lucky to have such a considerate and stalwart publisher. Carole Roos has edited the last three books at the Notre Dame Press. She has saved me from stylistic sins, both mortal and venial, and offered a number of substantive suggestions.

For the past several years, Rev. Theodore M. Hesburgh, C.S.C., President Emeritus of Notre Dame, has kindly passed along publications, reports, and articles about politics and communications. These items have been both helpful and much appreciated.

Thomas J. Stritch, Professor Emeritus of American Studies at Notre Dame and former editor of *The Review of Politics*, read the entire manuscript with characteristic care and duly noted places in need of revision or expansion.

Nancy Kegler deserves an author's applause for deciphering hundreds of handwritten pages, processing them into the computer, and then making all the subsequent changes in preparing the final version. She did all of this—as well as handle the American Studies office at Notre Dame—with good humor and professionalism. Two student assistants in American Studies, Mary K. Schultze (1992–1993) and Amanda Clinton (1993–1994), provided the answers to many questions they were asked to research.

On the home front, Judith Roberts Schmuhl and Michael Robert Schmuhl cheerfully endured another presidential campaign, along with the domestic disruptions resulting from it. And, alas, the lame refrain— "Sorry, but all of this will be over soon"—was used for another full year after the election as this volume took shape. I'm more than grateful for their forbearance and understanding.

Doing a book like this requires reading, watching, and listening to the media coverage of American political life. In many ways, print and broadcast sources provide the primary material requiring daily assessment. Many of the quotations used here come directly either from newspapers or magazines or from transcriptions of television or radio programs.

Of immense value to understanding the role of the different forms of popular communications in the political year of 1992 is the series of reports, *The Media and Campaign '92*, published by The Freedom Forum Media Studies Center at Columbia University. Center director Everette E. Dennis and his colleagues in "the Research Group" provide informed and comprehensive analysis, despite journalistic rather than academic deadlines. Three of the reports—*Covering the Presidential Primaries, An Uncertain Season: Reporting in the Post-primary Period*, and *The Homestretch: New Politics. New Media. New Voters?*—appeared during the campaign, and *The Finish Line: Covering the Campaign's Final Days* came out in January 1993. These four reports offer such in-depth and reasoned commentary that one wonders about their impact on the media throughout the campaign and for the future.

The Twentieth Century Fund also produced timely assessments of the political-communications environment. The book *The New News v. The Old News: The Press and Politics in the 1990s* (1992) with essays by Jay Rosen and Paul Taylor, is thoughtful throughout, and *1-800-President* (1993) is a cogent interpretation of television's involvement in the primaries and general election of 1992. Papers by Kathleen Hall Jamieson, Ken Auletta, and Thomas E. Patterson amplify points that are made by the "Task Force on Television and the Campaign of 1992."

Popular books with valuable background about the 1992 race began appearing during the summer and fall of 1993. Well worth consulting are *Strange Bedfellows: How Television and the Presidential Candidates Changed American Politics, 1992* by Tom Rosenstiel (New York: Hyperion, 1993); *Mad as Hell: Revolt at the Ballot Box, 1992* by Jack W. Germond and Jules Witcover (New York: Warner Books, 1993), and *On the Line: The New Road to the White House* by Larry King with Mark Stencel (New York: Harcourt Brace, 1993). Rosenstiel received access to the planning and activity at ABC, and he focuses on the way that network handled the coverage of the 1992 campaign. Germond and Witcover continue in the tradition established by Theodore H. White in *The Making of the President, 1960*, chronicling the campaign from the dual vantage point of what we saw occur and what took place behind the scenes. King's book recounts his involvement in the political year of 1992 and the emergence of new outlets of communication for candidates seeking high office.

Why Americans Hate Politics by E. J. Dionne, Jr. (New York: Simon and Schuster, 1991) played an important role in helping politicians, journalists, academics, and citizens think about the condition of our political life as the campaign took shape and then unfolded. Dionne's argument about the "politics of false choices" has become an often-heard, if not always attributed, principle of political discourse. The interest and involvement in the 1992 race didn't really reflect hatred of politics so much as anger and frustration at the way politics is now played in the United States. Institutional and procedural reforms would help the public to have a better attitude about their political life. Samuel L. Popkin's *The Reasoning Voter: Communication and Persuasion in Presidential Campaigns* (Chicago: University of Chicago Press, 1991) effectively shows that most voters don't have a vast amount of civic knowledge of the textbook variety. They, however, take telling "cues" from politicians, interpreting those cues in a continuing process of acceptance and rejection. Instead of dwelling on civic ignorance or a lack of close attention to political issues, Popkin concentrates on the relationship between what citizens comprehend from their experience and what they expect government to do.

Gil Troy's *See How They Ran: The Changing Role of the Presidential Candidate* (New York: The Free Press, 1991) documents the changes, continuities, and contradictions of pursuing the White House from the time of George Washington to that of George Bush. Although he describes individual campaigns in detail, Troy is more concerned with showing larger patterns and the paradoxes of seeking the presidency. In *What It Takes: The Way to the White House* (New York: Random House, 1992), Richard Ben Cramer closely examines the lives of six candidates who ran for president in 1988— George Bush, Bob Dole, Michael Dukakis, Gary Hart,

Joe Biden, and Richard Gephardt. The profiles are frequently riveting, and Cramer shows how the electoral system is out of control. Seeking the White House is an almost dehumanizing experience, and to win is to lose your life as you know it. That the book is 1,047 pages long and ends *before* the political conventions in 1988 might indicate the wealth of reporting and detail.

The economic condition of the United States is an influential factor in creating the political mood of the time. *America: What Went Wrong?* (Kansas City: Andrews and McMeel, 1992) by Donald L. Barlett and James B. Steele is a primer of the discontent that pervaded 1992 and continued after the election. Barlett and Steele blame Washington lawmakers and Wall Street dealmakers for working together at the expense of those in the middle class. Clever manipulation of government rules benefit the moneyed class, and politicians receive rewards in the form of campaign contributions and other acts of appreciation. In *Boiling Point: Democrats, Republicans, and the Decline of Middle-Class Prosperity* (New York: Random House, 1993), Kevin Phillips argues that the threat to the middle class is so important it places in jeopardy America's standing as an economic and political power. Phillips appropriates Paul Kennedy's thesis in *The Rise and Fall of the Great Powers: Economic Change and Military Conflict from 1500 to 2000* (New York: Random House, 1987) and makes a cautionary appeal of what's at stake for the nation—and world—should the middle class continue to lose its vigor and strength.

Given the rapidly changing territory of new communications, newspapers and magazines rather than books are frequently more useful and instructive. However, Bill McKibben's *The Age of Missing Information* (New York: Random House, 1992) is a provocative study, with a definite point of view, of the value (or lack thereof) of having an abundance of media choice. In *Life After Television:*

The Coming Transformation of Media and American Life (New York: W. W. Norton, 1992) George Gilder explains how in future years the television will become "the telecomputer" and what this technology will mean in economic, political, social, and cultural terms. W. Russell Neuman's *The Future of the Mass Audience* (Cambridge and New York: Cambridge University Press, 1991) is a cogent, methodically presented analysis of what the new forms of communication will be able to offer the public. Interestingly, Neuman does not see the world changing or the habits of media usage varying greatly as a result of the so-called information revolution.

Demography might—or might not—mean destiny, and studies of population trends point to racial and ethnic composition in America of the twenty-first century that is considerably different from what's existed in this century. Understanding the future will require familiarity with the past, and Ronald Takaki's *A Different Mirror: A History of Multicultural America* (Boston: Little, Brown and Company, 1993) is a valuable work for establishing a foundation of the necessary knowledge to interpret the diversity of this nation. In *The Disuniting of America: Reflection on a Multicultural Society* (New York: W. W. Norton, 1992), Arthur M. Schlesinger, Jr., provides a bracing warning that extremism in the defense of diversity could, ultimately, endanger the sense of common purpose that has helped unite Americans throughout the history of our democracy.